FIELD GUIDE TO
Disney's
ANIMAL
KINGDOM®
THEME PARK

For Disney Editions
Editorial Director: Wendy Lefkon
Senior Editor: Sara Baysinger
Associate Editor: Rich Thomas

For Roundtable Press, Inc.
Directors: Susan E. Meyer, Marsha Melnick, Julie Merberg
Editor: John Glenn
Editorial Assistant: Carrie Glidden
Design: Richard J. Berenson
          Berenson Design & Books, Ltd.
Production: Steven Rosen
Principal photography: Susan E. Meyer
Animal text: Lois Spritzer
Horticulture text: Debbie Mola
Manufacturing consultant: Bill Rose

Photography credits are found on page 151 and
constitute an extension of this copyright page.

ISBN 0-7868-8401-0
First Edition
2 4 6 8 10 9 7 5 3 1

FOREWORD

Even though I have been involved with DISNEY'S ANIMAL KINGDOM® PARK since 1992—six years before the park's 1998 opening—I am not exaggerating when I say that I am reminded daily why I am so proud of this park.

Spending even a few minutes, for example, watching the gorillas interacting with one another or seeing the tigers at play is a poignant reminder of what a privilege it is to be able to observe these incredible animals.

And the park's landscaping is a show in itself, which is no surprise, since DISNEY'S ANIMAL KINGDOM PARK has plants from every continent except Antarctica. The animals at our park love the plants just as much as the guests do—but the animals love eating and trampling them. What may be the first park that encourages the animals to eat the scenery creates all sorts of interesting challenges!

And I couldn't imagine not adding how proud I am of the people who care for the park's animals, plants, and, of course, our guests. Not a day goes by when I am not amazed by their creativity, enthusiasm, and commitment. It is their passion for what they do that makes DISNEY'S ANIMAL KINGDOM PARK such an extraordinary place.

When guests visit DISNEY'S ANIMAL KINGDOM PARK, we want them to enjoy the wonders of our animal world, but we also want them to go away inspired by what they see and to become personally involved in conservation efforts in their own communities and in conserving wildlife and wild places around the world.

One way the WALT DISNEY WORLD® Resort supports conservation efforts is through the Disney Wildlife Conservation Fund, which promotes wildlife conservation worldwide by funding projects of scientists, educators, and organizations committed to preserving Earth's biodiversity. WALT DISNEY WORLD guests can contribute to the fund wherever they see the Disney Wildlife Conservation Fund logo.

The animals at DISNEY'S ANIMAL KINGDOM PARK are ambassadors for their counterparts in the wild, helping to communicate the importance of animal conservation and habitat preservation. I hope that this book on the animals and plants of DISNEY'S ANIMAL KINGDOM PARK brings inspiration and a new understanding of the diversity of life in the world and the role that people must play if the animals and their habitats are to survive.

Bob Lamb
Vice President
Disney's Animal Kingdom

CONTENTS

SPECIAL FEATURES

PANGANI
FOREST
EXPLORATION
TRAIL®

KILIMANJARO
SAFARIS®

WILDLIFE
EXPRESS TO
CONSERVATION
STATION®

AFRICA

HARAMBE
VILLAGE

SAFARI
VILLAGE®

THE TREE
OF LIFE®

CAMP
MINNIE-
MICKEY

THE OASIS

ENTRANCE
PLAZA

CONSERVATION STATION®

MAHARAJAH JUNGLE TREK

KALI RIVER RAPIDS

ASIA

DINOLAND U.S.A.®

CRETACEOUS TRAIL

THE OASIS

THE TREE OF LIFE

AFRICA

ASIA

DINOLAND U.S.A.

CONSERVATION STATION

THROUGHOUT

INDEX

YOUR PERSONAL GUIDE

DISNEY'S ANIMAL KINGDOM® PARK covers just over 500 acres and is the largest of Disney's theme parks. The African savanna of the KILIMANJARO SAFARIS® alone covers 100 acres. The theme park is home to approximately 4 million trees, plants, shrubs, vines, grasses, and ferns representing more than 3,000 species. These plants create an amazing environment for guests to visit, and they are also essential to the health and happiness of the animals living in the habitats.

This book is your personal guide to the animals and plants featured throughout the theme park. Carry it with you as you meander through the paths at The Oasis, The Tree of Life, PANGANI FOREST EXPLORATION TRAIL®, Maharajah Jungle Trek, Cretaceous Trail, and CONSERVATION STATION®, and refer to it when you travel on the KILIMANJARO SAFARIS vehicle though the African savanna. In fact, take it wherever you go and check off the boxes alongside the animal or plant names whenever you make a positive identification, like so:

☑◀ **Yellow-bellied Slider**
Trachemys scripta scripta

Use the color tabs on the right sides of the pages to locate the area you are visiting and find the photograph that matches what is before you. If you are looking for a specific plant or animal and want to know where to find it in the park and in the book, refer to the indexes at the back of this field guide.

The field guide will be the record you have kept of your visit to DISNEY'S ANIMAL KINGDOM PARK, a souvenir of what we hope will be a most memorable adventure.

THE OASIS

The Oasis opens your journey through DISNEY'S ANIMAL KINGDOM® PARK. And a splendid entry it is: enter the cool shade of this lush, fertile garden refuge growing in and around grottos, waterfalls, and glades. Here you will find a rich collection of orchids and unusual birds and animals from throughout the world. When you enter The Oasis, proceed to the left or right on the path, and don't overlook the small detours along the way that may contain surprising discoveries.

❏ ◀ **Yellow-bellied Slider**
Trachemys scripta scripta
Native to wetlands of the southeastern United States, the Yellow-bellied Slider is easy to spot. In addition to its distinctive yellow belly, it's a large turtle, sometimes reaching 10 inches when fully grown. It grows slowly, though, and often does not reach adult size until it is eight or nine years old.

Scarlet Ibis ❑ ▶

Eudocimus ruber

The first creature to catch your eye will probably be the brilliant Scarlet Ibis. This striking wading bird was once hunted almost to extinction for its intensely colored feathers, but thanks to conservation efforts, the Scarlet Ibis is now thriving in the wild. You can enjoy a spectacular show of scarlet feathers when viewing these colorful birds, which live in colonies that range from 50 to 50,000 pairs along the coastal regions of northern South America. Even more spectacular is seeing the scarlet streak they form in flight—usually in V-formation. They even feed in large numbers: up to 70 birds sometimes dig together in the mud for crabs, mollusks, insects, and worms.

FUN FACT: All species of ibis have long, down-curving beaks for probing food out of the mud and soil.

Two-toed Sloth

(see CONSERVATION STATION®, *page 115)*

WADING BIRDS

Many wading birds are large and have long, thin legs. Their necks are also long and flexible so that they can reach into the water with their bills to catch aquatic prey. The long legs of wading birds seem to bend backward, but the "knee" joint is in fact an ankle. The leg below the joint should be properly considered as the foot, and what is often mistaken for the feet are really toes.

African Spoonbill ❑ ▲

Platalea alba

Sharing the habitat with the Scarlet Ibis is the African Spoonbill, a wading bird easily identified by its spoon-shaped bill and its pink, almost red, legs. In fact, this is the only white, red-legged member of the spoonbill family in Africa. In the wild, African Spoonbills travel in large groups, sometimes more than 250 pairs, although they feed in smaller numbers (about 10 birds). As spoonbills wade in shallow waters they "sweep" their bill from side to side, straining small items from the water and snapping at small fish and frogs. And when they take to the sky, spoonbills often fly in V-formation.

FUN FACT: Want to know when spoonbills are courting? Listen for the sound of bill-clacking—that's a sure prelude to mating.

Black-necked Swan ❑ ▼
Cygnus melanocoryphus

Often swimming near the Scarlet Ibis at the entrance to The Oasis, the Black-necked Swan has a white body and a large red knob at the base of its bill. It is one of the smallest swans. In the wild, the Black-necked Swan navigates swamps, marshes, lagoons, shallow lakes, and coastlines of South America and thrives on pondweeds, algae, and aquatic insects. Black-necked Swans breed in the spring, building their nests in reed beds. They carry their young "piggyback" to protect them from cold water and from possible predators.

FUN FACT: Like all swans, the Black-necked species shows no distinction in plumage between male (cob) and female (pen). But there is a way to distinguish them: the female is slightly smaller than the male. The juveniles (cygnets) have no knobs on their bills.

Babirusa ❑ ▼
Babyrousa babyrussa

These highly endangered Asian mammals resemble pigs, though some researchers think they're more closely related to the hippopotamus. The Babirusa has upper teeth or tusks that grow through the muzzle, and lower canines that protrude from the sides of the mouth. In fact, the upper canines of the male (boar) can measure up to a foot in length. These teeth are too brittle to be of use as weapons, but it is thought that their value is in providing a protective screen in front of the upper parts of the Babirusa's face. Babirusas are solitary creatures, living alone or in small family groups. They feed on fruits, fungi, and leaves, and can crack open the shells of hard nuts with their impressive teeth. The Babirusa habitat is located next to the Sulphur-crested Cockatoo.

FUN FACT: Indonesian natives say the tusks of this animal look like the antlers of a deer, hence its name Babirusa, which means "pig deer."

Military Macaw ❏ ▲
Ara militaris militaris
The Military Macaw is located in The Oasis near the Giant Anteater. At first glance, this macaw looks like an army sergeant feathered in olive green, hence its name. But take into account its red forehead, rose face striped with black and green, blue flight feathers, and maroon tail feathers, and it's totally out of uniform. Observed in pairs or flocks high in the mountains of northwestern South America, Military Macaws feed on fruits and nuts, and occasionally they eat clay.

Hyacinth Macaw ❏ ▲
Anodorhynchus hyacinthinus
An endangered species, the splendidly colored Hyacinth Macaw is the largest of the macaw species. It has cobalt-blue plumage that runs to a dark gray at the underside of its tail, and a yellow ring around the eye and lower mandible. At home in the tropical rain forests of interior Brazil, these macaws feed on seeds, palm fruits, and nuts. You will find the Hyacinth Macaw in the habitat opposite the Rhinoceros Iguana.
FUN FACT: Although the Hyacinth Macaw appears to be blue, in fact there is no blue pigment in its feathers. It is the structure of the feather that produces the blue cast.

PSITTACIFORMES
Pronounced "sit-AH-siforms," Psittaciformes is the scientific name of the distinctive order of birds that includes 340-plus species of parrots, cockatoos, macaws, and lories, of which 70 are listed as endangered. All are adapted to living in trees, where they use both beak and feet for climbing. Their feet have two toes pointing forward and two pointing backward to give them a vice-like grip. The feet also serve as "hands" to husk and hold seeds. Their bills are distinctive, curved in such a way that the lower fits neatly into the upper when the beak is closed, and their muscles are very flexible, giving them the strength to crack open the hardest nutshells. Psittaciformes live in colorful and noisy groups throughout the tropics.

Scarlet Macaw ❏ ◀

Ara macao

It's hard to miss these macaws in their native habitats. Their bright scarlet and yellow plumage and their harsh, metallic screeches add splashes of color and sound effects to the forests of Central America and central and northern South America. They are also familiar sights to arm-chair travelers because Scarlet Macaws are often shown on the covers of travel brochures that present the wonders of South America. Ironically, the Scarlet Macaw's popularity has become its downfall, as collectors have placed it in danger of extinction in Central America.

FUN FACT: Of all the macaws, the Scarlet has the longest tail feathers.

COCKATOOS

Cockatoos belong to a small group of Psittaciformes that inhabit Australia, New Guinea, and neighboring islands. Cockatoos are easily recognized by the crest of erectile feathers on the head.

Sulphur-crested Cockatoo ❏ ◀

Cacatua galerita

The cockatoo is located in the habitat next to the Babirusa (see page 11). Sulphur-crested Cockatoos originate from Australasia. A good-natured and long-lived pet (one of this species, the oldest bird in captivity in the world, lived to the ripe old age of 82), the cockatoo is wary in the wild; a flock designates a sentry that perches in a tree and warns of oncoming predators by issuing a loud screech.

FUN FACT: The Sulphur-crested Cockatoo's distinctive yellow crest is more than simply an adornment. The crest is used to show fear, aggression, or excitement.

Giant Anteater ❑ ▶
Myrmecophaga tridactyla

True to its name, the Giant Anteater measures about 9 feet from head to tail, and its tongue can reach an additional 24 inches in length. In the wild it can consume 30,000 termites in a single day. Found in the swampy areas and savannas of Central and South America, the Giant Anteater spends most of its day sniffing the ground for food. Although it has no teeth and its eyesight is poor, the anteater has an excellent sense of smell, and its huge nails can open a termite mound with one swipe. Anteaters at DISNEY'S ANIMAL KINGDOM® PARK consume a nutritionally complete dry mixture, with fruit for enrichment, and insects.

FUN FACT: The anteater can retract its tongue up to 160 times a minute as it retrieves insects from small crevices.

Rhinoceros Iguana ❑ ▼
Cyclura cornuta

Its name isn't intended to indicate its size. The Rhinoceros Iguana is so dubbed because the protuberance on the end of its snout resembles the rhino's horn. Like other cold-blooded animals, the Rhinoceros Iguana maintains its body heat by basking in the sun. Its diet consists mainly of plants but can include insects and other invertebrates. The Rhinoceros Iguana is located opposite the Hyacinth Macaw.

FUN FACT: Rhinoceros Iguanas have the perfect coloring for survival in their woodland home. Their color—dusky gray or olive green—provides great camouflage.

Parma Wallaby ❑ ▼
Macropus parma

One of the smallest of all wallabies (males weigh 13 pounds, females 10), the Parma has strong hindquarters and an equally strong tail, perfect for jumping; the tail also acts as a third leg, for balance. Wallabies are marsupials—that is, their young develop in a pouch. The newborn Parma Wallaby leaves the birth canal, makes its way to its mother's pouch, finds one of the mammae (nipples), and feeds there until it is about 210 days old. Nocturnal and solitary, wallabies congregate only at feeding sites, where they dine on grasses and herbs. Parma Wallabies are found in eastern New South Wales in Australia. At DISNEY'S ANIMAL KINGDOM PARK, the wallaby lives with the Sulphur-crested Cockatoo.

FUN FACT: In order to avoid the thorns and brambles of their forest homes, wallabies move around with their arms tucked close to their bodies.

WALLABIES
The name "wallaby" is reserved for smaller species of kangaroos in which the feet of the adult are less than 10 inches long. There are about 50 species of wallabies.

Tufted Deer ❏ ▶

Elaphodus cephalophus

If you take a slight detour from the path opposite the Giant Anteater and the Two-toed Sloth, you will come upon the Tufted Deer. You can recognize it by the black-brown tuft on its forehead, which tends to conceal its small antlers. The Tufted Deer has deep chocolate-brown upperparts, gray head and neck, and white-tipped ears. When this deer runs, its tail flops with every bounce, displaying a white underside. Its spine-like hairs give this animal a shaggy appearance.

FUN FACT: These deer use hearing, smelling, and sight to detect danger. Their vocal communication is more or less limited to bleats or alarm barks.

Reeves Muntjac ❏ ▼

Muntiacus reevesi reevesi

Opposite the Babirusa and cockatoo you'll find the Reeves Muntjac. Also known as the Barking Deer (it emits a bark-like sound when threatened), the chestnut-colored Reeves Muntjac is found in the woodlands and forests of southern China and Taiwan. Its "bark" lets predators know they have been spotted. For additional protection, the muntjac has elongated, tusk-like upper canines that curve outward from the lips. The animal produces a clicking sound by moving its tongue against these small tusks. Muntjacs subsist on grasses, leaves, and shoots, although they also eat pheasants and other small animals.

FUN FACT: Muntjacs are such accomplished hunters that they can find and consume trapped pheasants before the humans who set the traps arrive on the scene.

Bufflehead ❑ ▶

Bucephala albeola

Buffleheads are the smallest of the North American diving ducks and among the smallest and swiftest of all waterfowl anywhere in the world. To attract females, the male (drake) bobs his head up and down and displays his diving skills. The Bufflehead is one of the few ducks that keeps the same mate for several years.

White-faced Whistling-Duck ❑ ◀

Dendrocygna viduata

Highly vocal, whistling-ducks announce their presence with a melodious, three-note whistle (not a quack); they sound a single note when they sense danger. This species has a black-and-white head, white face, and chestnut breast. It raises and shakes its head before taking flight and whistles for a short time after take-off. Feeding occurs mostly at night, when the ducks swim and dive for their food. (They can stay submerged for 5 to 10 seconds.) Courtship consists partly of mutual preening; both male and female build the nest, and the female lays up to 13 eggs.

Chiloe Wigeon ❑ ▶

Anas sibilatrix

Native to South America, the Chiloe is heavier than other wigeons, and both sexes look alike. Male wigeons whistle, and females quack. Although Chiloe Wigeons spend most of their time in the water, they feed mainly on land. Females lay between five and eight eggs, which hatch after a 26-day incubation period. Breeding time is usually August and September. The male (drake) wigeon helps care for the chicks after they hatch.

DUCKS

Because ducks are swimmers they have certain features in common: they have wide bodies for buoyancy and webbed feet for paddling; most bills are long and flat; their necks tend to be proportionately long; their eggs are pale without spots; and their hatchlings are covered with soft, fluffy down. Most ducks are poor walkers because their feet are set far back on the body, for efficient swimming. Ducks tend to be as expert in flight as they are in swimming. They can take off from the water and fly swiftly, covering great distances in migration. Apart from these generic features, however, ducks are very distinctive in their specific features and behaviors.

Javan Tree Duck ❑ ▲
Dendrocygna javanica
The smallest of the whistling-ducks (it's also known as the Lesser Whistling-Duck), the Javan Tree Duck inhabits the tropical jungles and swamps of lowland India, Thailand, Sri Lanka, Pakistan, and China. These ducks build their nests in tree cavities, some using hollows as high up as 100 feet.

Hooded Merganser ❑ ▲
Lophodytes cucullatus
Most mergansers have fan-shaped crests, but that of the Hooded species is the most distinctive. The Hooded is also the smallest of the merganser species and the only merganser native to North America. Making their home within the hollows of dead trees or in secluded pools and lakes, they are not as social as diving ducks. The Hoodeds tend to fly more than most mergansers, moving fast and low. Primarily fish eaters, they will also readily take frogs, tadpoles, crustaceans, and small mollusks.

Indian Spotbill ❑ ▲
Anas poecilorhyncha poecilorhyncha
The Indian Spotbill gets its name from the orange and yellow markings on its bill. The male (drake) has a bright orange patch at the base of its bill that swells and becomes more colorful during the breeding season. Not a strong flier, the Indian Spotbill is fairly sedentary, content to feed on the aquatic insects, worms, water snails, and vegetation indigenous to its habitat: the jheels (pools, marshes, or lakes) of the Indian subcontinent.

Mandarin ❑ ▲
Aix galericulata
The rather small Mandarin duck is recognizable by the orange-gold "sails" in its wings and its dark red beak (the female has green flight feathers and small white marks around her eyes). The species migrates seasonally but always seeks out lakes, rivers, and marshes. Mandarins nest in tree cavities or on the ground, producing up to 12 eggs that hatch in 30 days. Because the Mandarin is monogamous, the Chinese regard it as a symbol of marital fidelity.

17

Bahama Pintail ❑ ▶

Anas bahamensis rubrirostris

The Bahama Pintail is also known as the White-cheek Pintail because of the white markings on its head. These splendidly colored birds are found in mangrove swamps and lagoons in Brazil, Argentina, Peru, and Chile. Bahama Pintails are sedentary birds, content to feed on the local seeds, leaves, and aquatic plants. They build their nests on the ground in thick vegetation and tree roots located close to water.

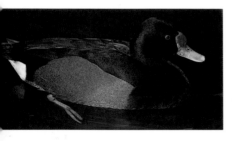

Rosybill Pochard ❑ ▲

Netta peposaca

The shallow, freshwater swamps, marshes, and lakes of South America are home to the Rosybill Pochard. During the breeding season the knob on the male's bill increases in color intensity and size. The female Rosybill does not always use her own nest. Sometimes she will lay her eggs on top of another duck's eggs. In this way broods may merge, resulting in large numbers of ducklings tended by a single female duck.

Ringed Teal ❑ ▲

Callonetta leucophrys

Rarely wandering far from their wetland habitats in South America, Ringed Teals feed on the roots and leaves of both aquatic and ground-based plants. The males and females form solitary pairs, and the males assist in building the nests on the ground and in rearing the young. Like most ducks in the Southern Hemisphere, male Ringed Teals retain their breeding plumage all year.

Ruddy Duck ❑ ▼

Oxyura jamaicensis

Nicknamed the "Butterball" (for its chubby shape) or the "Stifftail" (for its long, firm tail feathers), the Ruddy Duck prefers warm climates and stable water levels and is at home in the vegetated prairie marshes of North America and the West Indies. Like Rosybill Pochards, Ruddy Ducks often lay their eggs in the same nests as other females. Since the average female hatches up to 10 eggs, multiple families can produce large numbers of ducklings.

Radjah Shelduck ❑ ▲
Tadorna radjah

The wetlands, tidal mud flats, and rivers of Indonesia (the Moluccas Islands) and Guinea are home to these handsome shelducks. They have a white face, crown, neck, and breast; their bills are pink, their shoulders are brown or black, and there is a distinctive black band across their breasts. Radjah Shelducks spend their days resting in wooded areas and their nights in shallow water, sweeping their bills from side to side beneath the surface in search of small mollusks.

Puna Teal ❑ ▶
Anas puna

The Puna Teal is distinctive because of its striking, hyacinth-blue bill. Puna Teals

inhabit the Andean Highlands (up to 10,000 feet) of Peru, Bolivia, and Chile. The sexes are similar in appearance; the female is slightly smaller than the male.

Florida Chicken Turtle ❑ ▲
Deirochelys reticularia chrysea

The Florida Chicken Turtle is medium-size, and its oval shell has a reticulated pattern of yellow lines. It has an extremely long neck that equals the length of its shell. It is usually found in ditches and ponds rather than in moving water. Because it is the thinnest-shelled turtle in Florida, it is unlikely to inhabit large bodies of water with alligators.
FUN FACT: Adult females are larger than adult males, and their shells are more steeply domed.

PLANT AND ANIMAL NAMES

There are hundreds of thousands of plants and animals throughout the world, and until the 18th century their names were often vague and confusing. In 1735, with the publication of his *Systema Naturae*, Swedish naturalist Carolus Linnaeus introduced the "binomial system" (two-name system)—the first scientific system for classifying and naming plants and animals. Under the binomial system, botanists classified the plant kingdom into a hierarchy of groups, including family, and subdividing further into genus, species, cultivars, and natural hybrids. Zoologists classified animals as to family, genus, species, and subspecies (or race; when an animal's Latin name has three words, the third word is the subspecies name).

Linnaeus presented his system in Latin, the international language of science in his day. The widespread use of Latin meant that scientific clarity and precision could be preserved across international boundaries. Because the system for classifying plants is more complex than the one for animals, the explanation that follows focuses on plants.

FAMILY

Every plant and every animal belongs to a family, members of which share certain very broad characteristics that may not even be visible. Orchidaceae, for example, contains many plants that seem to bear little resemblance to other members of the family.

GENUS

A family is divided into groups of more closely related species. Each such group is called a *genus* (the plural of *genus* is *genera*). The first part of a plant's scientific name is the genus, and it is

Heliconia bihai

Heliconia stricta

Heliconia psitticorum

Heliconia rostrata

always capitalized and italicized. *Heliconia,* for example, is a genus; the plants in this genus have several basic characteristics in common with all other *Heliconias.*

SPECIES
The second name is the species name, which always appears in lowercase and italicized. In the *Heliconia* genus, for example, in this book you will see *Heliconia rostrata, Heliconia psitticorum, Heliconia stricta,* and *Heliconia bihai.* As a shortcut, once the genus name has been given in full, these may be referred to as *H. rostrata, H. psitticorum, H. stricta,* and *H. bihai.* The heading that includes all four is written as *Heliconia spp.* (species).

*Rhododendron
'Jock's Cairn'*

CULTIVARS
Horticulturists continually seek to create even further variations, or cultivars, within species. Breeding programs are conducted to create plants with features that improve on the parent species. To signify that a plant is a cultivar, the breeder gives it a name in the form of a word or phrase; this name is capitalized, written with single quotes, and not italicized. *Rhododendron* 'Jock's Cairn' was named by Jock Brydon, a horticulturist who spent much of his life breeding and cross-breeding vireya rhododendrons.

HYBRIDS
The cross-breeding of one species with another, or even one genus with another, creates hybrids. Most hybrids are indicated with an x placed between the two names. If the cross-breeding occurs in nature, the hybrid is indicated this way: *Clerodendron* x *speciosm* (with the main words italicized). Most hybrids are man-made, however, and this is

Phragmipedium
Eric Young

indicated with the first word in italic and the second part not italicized: *Phragmipedium* Eric Young. With some groups of plants, particularly orchids, there has been much hybridization among genera, creating bigeneric hybrids. For example, when the genus *Cattleya* is crossed with the genus *Laelia,* the resulting genus is *Laeliocattleya.* Orchids have been so extensively hybridized that it's not uncommon to find plants that are the combination of as many as seven or eight or even more genera.

COMMON NAMES
It is often more convenient to refer to species by their common names, but beware. Not all plants have common names. Some have several common names. Sometimes more than one species share the same name. And common names for the same species can vary from one country to another, even if these countries are all English-speaking. The same can be true with animals, but their common names are generally so much more familiar than their scientific names that this book gives the common names of animals first.

Billbergia pyramidalis 'Muriel Waterman'

Typical Bromeliad

Aristolochia grandiflora ❑ ▲

Pelican Flower or Dutchman's Pipe

The *Aristolochia* genus contains more than 300 species, including many climbers that range in size from 36 inches to 30 feet. Native to Central America, this vining plant has flowers that resemble the neck of a pelican or perhaps a pipe. The purple and green flowers can reach up to 6 inches or more in diameter, making it one of the largest and fastest-growing in the *Aristolochia* genus.

FUN FACT: The flowers are pollinated by flies, which the plant attracts by exuding the scent of carrion. The A. grandiflora *then traps the fly within the flower and keeps it inside until the plant is pollinated.*

Bromeliaceae spp. ❑ ▲

Bromeliad family

Native to South America and parts of Central America and the West Indies, the Bromeliaceae family includes many unusual-looking plants. Some of them are familiar, such as the pineapples (*Ananas* spp.) and Spanish Moss (*Tillandsia usneoides*), and some are not, such as many of the *Guzmania* and *Cryptanthus* species. Each member in this family has a cup at the base of its leaf. This cup usually stores water that the plant uses. Many of the bromeliads are epiphytic, meaning they need a host for support. The *Billbergia pyramidalis* 'Muriel Waterman' is native to Brazil and is one of the more rapidly growing of the vase-forming species. It is a species of "tank epiphyte," a plant perched on a tree with the bases of its leaves overlapping so that it can collect water that it uses between rains.

Burbidgea schizocheila ❑ ◄

Burbidgea is one of the many genera that make up the ginger family. *B. schizocheila* is native to Borneo and Malaysia. The terminal flower clusters of this plant are yellow-orange, making them easy to spot. The blooms also bear a slight resemblance to a bird.

Caryota mitis
Fishtail Palm ❑ ▲

What this palm resembles is no mystery after you read the common name. The Fishtail Palm is the only palm with bipinnate (double compound) leaves. Native to Myanmar, it can be found anywhere from sea level to 7,000 feet above sea level.

Cananga odorata ❑ ▲
Ilang-Ilang

A fast-growing evergreen tree native to Southeast Asia, the Pacific Islands, and Australia, the *Cananga odorata* has flowers that are displayed in clusters of extremely fragrant yellow pendants. As the bloom persists on the tree, the fragrance becomes even more intense.

Caryota urens ❑ ▶
Wine Palm or Toddy Palm

Native to India, Myanmar, and Malaysia, this appealing, single-stem species of *Caryota* is grown for timber and for a beverage called toddy. The drink

is made by cutting off the young flower heads and collecting the vitamin-rich, sugary sap that overflows from the cut. After setting fruit, the entire stem will die. The *C. urens* lives only about 30 years.

Medinilla magnifica ❑ ◀

This plant doesn't need a common name to describe it. *Magnifica* says it all—it certainly describes the large, showy flowers that come in either pink or white. *Medinilla magnifica* usually blooms year-round. It has a shrub form with four unusual, angled, square stems. *M. magnifica* grows epiphytically in areas of the South Pacific, Asia, and tropical Africa.

Clematis paniculata ❑ ▶

This *Clematis* is a woody climber native to New Zealand that shows fragrant white flowers from late spring to early summer. Its cultivation dates back to the 16th century, making it one of the oldest domesticated plants growing today.

Hydnophytum formicarium ❑ ▲

Ant Plant

The Latin name of this plant is intimidating and really doesn't tell you much. *Hydnophytum formicarium,* commonly known as the Ant Plant, is one of the members of the Rubiaceae family. Ant Plants are relatives of coffee plants and gardenias and are native to Malaysia and Indonesia. *FUN FACTS: This epiphyte (it needs a host for support) has hollow chambers with entrance holes that allow ants to enter. The ants live inside the plant, and their waste, which includes insect parts, is used by the plant as a source of nutrients.*

Lepanthes spp. ❑ ▲

Over 60 species of *Lepanthes* grow in moist tropical forests from Mexico to Brazil. One attribute that links these species is a well-developed aerial stem, known as the ramicaul, which is enclosed by many ribbed sheaths with dilated openings that are often warty in appearance. The flowers are very small and fragile and come in a variety of wild colors. *Lepanthes* are difficult to cultivate.

FERNS

The small spores you see on the underside of most fern leaves are called sori. If you examine them with a magnifying glass you will see that each is really a cluster of tiny spore cases, which are called sporangia. Ferns reproduce through the release of spores, but spores don't become plants easily, which may be why nature produces them in enormous quantities. When the spore cases open, the spores are sprayed into the air, like powder. People in ancient civilizations knew about spore dust and thought it had magical qualities. They believed it would make them invulnerable to enemies and increase their powers as lovers, among other benefits. They ate and drank the spore dust and doused themselves with it.

Platycerium wandae ❑ ◀
Queen Staghorn
All of the members of the *Platycerium* genus are common to the tropical rain-forest regions of the world. Many can grow as large as 6 feet in circumference and get so heavy that their sheer weight can drop them to the ground. There are two types of leaves on these plants, sterile fronds and fertile fronds. Sterile fronds are the rounded fronds mounded around the base of the plant that tend to resemble stag or elk horns. Fertile fronds are the spreading, usually pendant, fronds. Water from rainfall and nutrients, such as bird droppings or dead insects, are funneled to the root system.

Plumeria hybrid ❑ ▶
Frangipani
The flowers of this small to medium-size shrub range from all shades of pinks and reds to yellows and white. The fragrance of the blooms can be overpowering. Early morning or early evening tends to be the best time to catch a whiff. Native to the New World, this genus was named after

French botanist Charles Plumier, who made three voyages to the Caribbean in the 17th century. Two explanations have been given for the common name Frangipani. According to one, it is derived from a perfume created by an Italian family of the same name; another claims that the thick white latex that flows when the tree is cut reminded the French settlers in the Caribbean of *fragipanier,* or coagulated milk.
FUN FACT: During World War I, Thomas Edison experimented with the sap of the Frangipani in the hope of using it as a possible substitute for latex.

Mansoa alliaceum ❑ ◀
Garlic Vine
Garlic Vine is found native in the West Indies and Central America. It can often grow to a length of 20 to 30 feet. The blooms are most plentiful during the hottest months of the year, but *Mansoa alliaceum* can produce flowers every six weeks or so throughout the year. Often the blooms will be several different colors at once. The flower's colors fade as it ages, producing the multicolored effect.
FUN FACT: When the leaves and stems of this plant are crushed, they have a very strong smell that resembles garlic, hence the common name.

Rhododendron 'Jock's Cairn' ❑ ▲

Tropical Rhododendron

The name *Rhododendron* may call up images of the thick, leathery-leafed varieties popular in the northeastern United States, but this species is a tropical variety. 'Jock's Cairn' is named after Jock Brydon, a horticulturist who spent much of his life trying to introduce vireya rhododendrons into the United States. Most of his work was performed at the Strybing Arboretum in San Francisco. The 'Jock's Cairn' has funnel-shaped blooms that are pink-red with dark pink throats.

Stigmaphyllon ciliatum ❑ ▲

Golden Vine

Stigmaphyllon ciliatum is a woody vine native to the coastal areas of Central and South America. The plant is distinguished by its brilliant yellow flowers, which can be abundant with full sun.

Thunbergia grandiflora
Blue Sky Vine

Thunbergia grandiflora
'Alba'
White Sky Vine

Thunbergia spp. ❑ ▲

The *Thunbergia* genus consists of 90 to 100 species of mostly climbing vines and evergreen shrubs. They grow on the forest floor and in rocky areas, often climbing through the forest trees. *Thunbergia* species are named after an 18th-century Swedish botanist, Dr. Carl Peter Thunberg, who collected them in Africa, Madagascar, and Asia.

THE OASIS

Of all the areas in DISNEY'S ANIMAL KINGDOM® PARK, The Oasis probably contains the most exotic plants and flowering trees within its lush domain. Accents of bromeliads, orchids, Thunbergia, and Aristolochia abound in this fertile, garden refuge.

Orchids

Orchids are members of the Orchidaceae family, the largest plant family in the world, with between 25,000 and 30,000 species. A great variety are grown by hobbyists and commercial producers, who supply the orchids florists use for cut flowers and other floral arrangements. The United States and Canada have many native orchids. Native orchids usually inhabit cool bogs, sandy plains, and moist grasslands. Many of them are not showy, while others have prominent flowers.

Unfortunately, many species are now rare because of the destruction of their natural habitats. In nature, orchids live under such specific conditions that it is almost impossible for most gardeners to grow these plants. The commercial orchids that we purchase for our homes are of tropical origin. Most of these orchids are not difficult to grow but do require close attention.

Many orchids, like the *Dendrobium* species, are epiphytes. "Epiphyte" is a botanical term used to describe a plant that grows naturally on another plant, gaining support only from its host. Epiphytes obtain all their water needs from rain or moisture in the air. For this reason they are often called air plants. Epiphytes have evolved in the greatest numbers in the warm and humid tropics because growing conditions there are warm throughout the year. In the tropics, epiphytes thrive in all niches, from the full sun of the highest treetops to deep shade.

Other orchids are lithophytes, which means they grow on moss-covered boulders, often close to running water (*Phalaenopsis*, as shown on page 29, sometimes grow lithophytically), or "terrestrial" (like *Phaius tankervilleae*), which is a ground-growing orchid.

Aerides lawrenceae x ascocenda ❑ ▲
Foxtail Orchid

Brassia rex 'Christine' AM/AOS ❑ ▶
Spider Orchid

Cattleya labiata var. autumnalis ❑ ▲
Cattleya

Colmanara Wildcat ❑ ▲
Wildcat Orchid

Cymbidium Golden Elf 'Sundust' ❏ ▲

Dendrobium lasianthera ❏ ▲
Dendrobium

Dendrobium hybrid ❏ ▲
Dendrobium

Dendrobium nobile hybrid ❏ ▲
Dendrobium

Miltonia hybrid ❏ ▲
Pansy Orchid

Oncidium hybrid ❏ ▲
Butterfly Orchid

Paphiopedilum hybrid ❏ ◄
Lady Slipper Orchid

**Phragmipedium
Sorcerer's
Apprentice** ❑ ▲
Lady Slipper

Phalaenopsis ❑ ▲
hybrid
Moth Orchid

**Phragmipedium
besseae** ❑ ▲
Lady Slipper

**Phragmipedium
Eric Young** ❑ ▲
Lady Slipper

**Vanda coerulea
'Evelyn' FCC/AOS**
❑ ◀
Blue Orchid

**Vanda
hybrid**
❑ ▼
Vanda Orchid

Capybara ❑ ▲
Hydrochaeris hydrochaeris

The Capybara is the largest member of the rodent family, weighing about 110 to 130 pounds. Its body hair is long and coarse. At home in small herds located in and around the ponds, lakes, rivers, and swamplands of South America, the Capybara feeds on grasses that grow in or near the water. Social and non-aggressive, Capybaras travel in groups of about 20. In order to define its territory, the male secretes a white fluid from an oversize scent gland located on the top of its snout and rubs it on plant stems along its chosen boundaries. Although its barrel shape and short legs make it seem awkward on land, the Capybara is a good swimmer; its eyes are set high on the head to enable it to see while swimming.

FUN FACTS: The name "Capybara" means "Master of the Grasses." The mound-shaped bump on the top of the adult male's nose is called a morillo, *the Spanish word for "small hill."*

Cotton-top Tamarin ❑ ▶
Saguinus oedipus

The spiky white fur of the Cotton-top Tamarin is truly its crowning glory. At home in northwestern Colombia, these diminutive members of the monkey family weigh only 12 to 16 ounces at maturity. Their small size serves them well, allowing them to perch on thin tree limbs in search of food (fruits and flowers, insects, spiders, frogs, and lizards). They're also impressive athletes, able to leap across distances of about 10 feet.

THE TREE OF LIFE

From The Oasis area you'll enter the SAFARI VILLAGE® area, where you'll get your first clear view of the 140-foot Tree of Life. Stroll through the overhead buttress root system of this tree draped with vines and flowering accent plants. All around this beautiful tree you'll see animals that are truly extraordinary, including some very unusual storks living along the shoreline of the Discovery River.

Axis Deer ❏ ▶

Cervus axis axis
Native to India, Sri Lanka, and Nepal, the Axis Deer makes its home in grass-lands and open forests. These deer are also good swimmers and can cross water without difficulty. The small spots on the deer's fur allow it to blend into the woodland scene; the male's 2.5-foot-high, lyre-shaped, six-pointed antlers could proba-bly be mistaken for tree branches. In the wild, herds comprise mostly females, with only a few mature males. Females are very protective of their young, hiding them in high grasses and feeding them until they are able to travel with the herd. In the park, the Axis Deer shares space with the Red Kangaroo and the Greater Flamingo.
FUN FACT: Unlike many other species of deer, the adult Axis Deer can shed and regrow its antlers at any time of year.

Asian Small-clawed Otter ❏ ▼

Aonyx cinerea
Equally at home in water and on land, otters populate rivers, creeks, coastal waters, wetlands, and man-grove swamps, din-ing—not surprisingly—on crabs, fish, mollusks,

and frogs. The otter has sensitive and agile forepaws, good for feeling for food under mud or stones, and oversize cheek teeth, ideal for crushing the shells of their sea creature entrée. Otters travel in small family groups (4 to 12 animals); baby otters (whelps) open their eyes within 40 days and start to swim when they are 9 weeks old. The otters are located to the left of the Greater Flamingos.
FUN FACT: From overhead, you can see the otters moving about on land, but you can also step into an underwater viewing area to see how well they navigate in the water.

Kenya Crested Guinea Fowl ❏ ▲
Guttera pucherani

Providing a touch of color in the forests and savannas of their eastern African homeland, this colorful species has black plumage and a prominent black crest, grayish-blue head and neck, and red or yellow markings around the throat and eyes. It forages on the ground for plants, fruits, berries, and insects. To build a nest, this guinea fowl simply scratches the surface of the soil with its claws and covers its nest with dead leaves. The Kenya Crested Guinea Fowl is located near the Discovery River, sharing space with the storks.

FUN FACT: Often more than one female Kenya Crested Guinea Fowl will share the same nest.

East African Crowned Crane ❏ ▲
Balearica regulorum

The East African Crowned Crane shares space with the White Stork, Red Kangaroo, and Axis Deer. Its distinctive, brush-like, feathered crown provides this crane with perfect camouflage in the tall grass of marsh, lakeside, and riverbank habitats—which also yield the seeds, rice, insects, mollusks, and amphibians that comprise its diet. East African Crowned Cranes fly low to the ground. They produce an occasional purring sound when feeding or socializing, and honk when threatened. A monogamous species, African crowned cranes pair off for life. Their courtship ritual consists of a dance (hopping, jumping, and bowing) and a loud "unison call." Both male and female tend the nest.

FUN FACT: The East (gray-necked) and West (black-necked) African Crowned Cranes are the only cranes to roost in trees.

GUESTS AT DISNEY'S ANIMAL KINGDOM® PARK

Not all the animals that you see live permanently in this theme park. Some local natives—like the Great White Egret and the Black Duck—drop in from the wild and remain as guests.

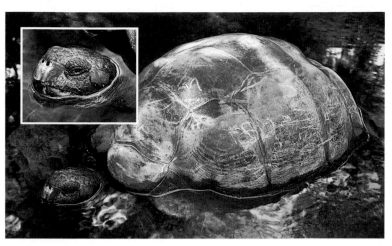

Galapagos Tortoise ❑ ▲
Geochelone elephantopus

There are several reasons these creatures can live 150 years: their hard shell, called a carapace, acts as camouflage and protection from predators; they are able to survive for long periods without food or water; and they're slow-moving animals, content to bask in the sun or cool themselves under the trees or wallow in the mud. In spite of these attributes, however, the Galapagos Tortoise has become highly endangered in its native habitat. They used to exist in massive numbers but have been reduced to extinction on some of the Galapagos Islands by competition for food with goats introduced by settlers and by slaughter for their meat. At The Tree of Life, the Galapagos Tortoise is located near the Capybara and shares space with the African Comb Duck.

FUN FACT: The location of the nest, and often the location of an egg within the nest, determines the gender of tortoise offspring: breeding areas with low temperatures yield mostly males, while warmer locations produce mostly females.

Greater Flamingo ❑ ▼
Phoenicopterus roseus

The graceful, pink Greater Flamingo is the largest in the flamingo family. It normally feeds with its head upside down and its bill underwater. The bill is designed as a strainer—it has ridges, called lamellae, that trap food particles while allowing water to pass through. In the wild, flamingos live in colonies of up to 20,000 pairs. Beautiful in flight, flamingos form a V-formation and have slow, graceful wingbeats. The Greater Flamingo is located near the entry to the Tree of Life.

FUN FACT: The flamingo has a thick tongue that can be retracted to pull water into its mouth and then pushed forward to force the water out and across the lamellae.

Green-winged Macaw ☐ ▲
Ara chloroptera

The Green-winged Macaw is often confused with the Scarlet Macaw because of the similar dark, crimson-red color of its head and neck feathers. The Green-winged Macaw, however, is much larger and has a green patch on each wing, followed by blue flight feathers. The cheeks have white patches with red stripes that, like those of the Scarlet Macaw, flush red when the bird is excited.

Blue-and-yellow Macaw ☐ ▲
Ara ararauna

Although this is one of the most colorful of birds, its plumage serves as excellent camouflage under the bright tropical sun of Central and South America. Its massive beak allows it to crush nut-shells (nuts, fruits, seeds, and berries are its preferred diet) and also helps it in climbing trees. Its toes point forward and backward and are ideal for grasping and gripping, and its long tail is great for balance. Since different foods are available during different seasons, macaws have been known to travel great distances for sustenance. The Blue-and-yellow Macaw lives near the Galapagos Tortoise at The Tree of Life.

Moluccan Cockatoo or Salmon-crested Cockatoo ☐ ◀
Cacatua moluccensis

The Moluccan Cockatoo is pink with a salmon crest and salmon on the underside of its wings. Moluccans have a harsh, raucous screech, but they are intelligent and highly social. They can live for 40 to 50 years. The Moluccan Cockatoo is located near the Ring-tailed Lemur.

Red Kangaroo ❑ ▼
Macropus rufus rufus

Found only in the central region of Australia, the Red Kangaroo is the largest of the marsupials (pouched mammals) and the most numerous of kangaroos. Usually the male kangaroo is red; the female and the young are bluish gray. A single offspring is born (generally in January) and remains in the pouch for nine months. No bigger than a human thumb at birth, the adult Red Kangaroo grows taller than a man.

Grazing on grass and shoots, Red Kangaroos will travel as far as 100 miles for food, and are able to move at up to 40 miles per hour. At high speeds they may jump almost 10 yards repeatedly. By comparison, Carl Lewis, the Olympic long-jumper, can jump 9 yards—and only once at a time.

FUN FACTS: In Australian kangaroo-speak, the male is called a boomer, the female a blue flier, and the juvenile a joey. A group of kangaroos is called a mob.

Ring-tailed Lemur ❑ ◄
Lemur catta

Found only on the island of Madagascar, the Ring-tailed Lemur is a cousin to the monkey and the ape. Ring-tails live in groups of up to 30, with the female as the dominant member. Suckling lemurs—even those orphaned from other groups—can be fed by any milk-producing female. The lemur's tail is longer than its body (approximately 23 inches for the tail, 16 inches for the body). More than just a striped appendage, the tail is raised as a warning to other lemurs that danger is approaching.

FUN FACTS: The name "lemur"—from the Latin word for ghost—is appropriate: look at this animal's big eyes and listen to its haunting howl.

Abdim's or White-bellied Stork ❑ ▲
Ciconia abdimii
Roosting on trees, cliffs, and sometimes the rooftops of huts, these black-and-white birds prefer to settle near water on open grassland but can also adapt to semi-desert regions. The Abdim's Stork breeds in May, nesting with other species, and producing two or three eggs that it incubates for about a month. Its diet consists of locusts, caterpillars, and crickets—with an occasional mouse or aquatic animal.
FUN FACT: The oldest Abdim's Stork in captivity lived more than 21 years.

Woolly-necked Stork ❑ ▲
Ciconia episcopus
Mostly glossy black (except for its white neck and lower belly), the Woolly-necked Stork sports a distinctive black skullcap. Feeding on locusts, grasshoppers, mollusks, crabs, and frogs in the wet grasslands and open forests of tropical Africa, these birds forage while walking. Although they have a hard time getting off the ground— they have to run a bit before taking off—Woolly-necks are accomplished, even acrobatic, fliers once they are in the air. They can soar, tumble, and dive at steep angles.

White Stork ❑ ▶
Ciconia ciconia
A symbol of fertility, the White Stork is reputed to deliver new babies to humans, making it the best-known of the stork species. Keeping true to its parental reputation, the White Stork is monogamous. The male stork arrives at his old nest and takes up his station to await the return of his mate. Once reunited, the male and female jointly rebuild their nest, taking turns incubating their eggs and feeding their young. The White Stork migrates each year from northern Europe to Africa. Conservation of these birds requires efforts by all the nations where the birds rest en route. Without adequate habitats, the White Storks will not survive.

FUN FACT: As the White Stork pairs rebuild their nests over the years, the nests can reach enormous proportions. Some have been known to measure 8 feet across and 8 feet deep, and to weigh more than 100 pounds.

Painted Stork ❏ ▶

Mycteria leucocephala

Its head is orange, its bill yellow, and its legs pink, but the black-and-white-checkered pattern of its plumage is this stork's main distinction. Its feet and beak are prime feeding tools: the feet stir up the bottom of shallow waters as the bird searches for food, and the beak (half-opened when feeding) scoops up the fish that are the mainstay of its diet. The impressive bill is also used in defending territories, as the stork flies aggressively over intruders, snapping its beak.

FUN FACT: During breeding season, the tail feathers of the Painted Stork become intensely pink, which explains its name.

Saddle-billed Stork ❏ ◀

Ephippiorhynchus senegalensis

Both male and female Saddle-billed Storks begin to form a crimson naked spot on their chests at or after the age of three years. The difference between male and female is apparent: the male has dark brown eyes and two yellow wattles at the base of his bill; the female is smaller and has bright yellow eyes. These basically non-migrating birds leave their home territory—in the marshes, wet grasslands, and edges of rivers and lakes in tropical Africa—only in search of better feeding sites.

STORKS AND SPOONBILLS

Storks and spoonbills have a number of features in common: all are characterized by long, slender, featherless legs and short, slightly webbed toes that are tipped with blunt claws. The shape of the bill may vary from species to species, but in all cases it has sharp cutting edges. One sound both groups make is a clattering of the beak. Although protected almost everywhere, storks and spoonbills are diminishing in number, primarily because their marshy habitats are drying up or being destroyed by human development.

Roseate Spoonbill ❑ ▲
Ajaja ajaja
The Roseate is the only pink-colored member of the spoonbill family. Once hunted nearly to extinction for its plumage, the Roseate Spoonbill has regained some but not all of its former numbers. Spoonbills forage on small fish, water beetles, shrimp, and some plants, including sedge roots and fibers. When foraging, they move their bill back and forth through the water and along muddy river bottoms in wide arcs; sometimes—probably if the tidbit looks good enough—they will immerse the entire head and part of the neck. Favoring the southeastern United States and the West Indies, Roseate Spoonbills make their home in tidal ponds and mangrove swamps; less frequently, they live inland, in pools, marshes, and rice fields.

FUN FACT: Male Roseates have a predominate dark pink stripe on each side of the body that becomes more distinct during mating season.

Silver Teal ❑ ▶
Anas versicolor
Though named for their silver-gray flanks, these colorful birds' most prominent features are their multihued feathers (white and metallic bronze-green) and their long, light-blue and orange bills. The Silver Teal feeds on seeds, insect larvae, and shrimp and clams in the shallow wetlands and marshes  of its South American homeland. During breeding season, pairs often produce up to four broods.

African Comb Duck ❑ ▲
Sarkidiornis melanotos
The African Comb Duck has a dark back with metallic violet, purple, bronze, and green coloring. The male has a fleshy knob at the base of the bill. Found in Africa, Asia, and South America, comb ducks travel more than 2,200 miles when migrating. They graze on land on seeds and grain, and in water on aquatic plants and invertebrates. They build their nests in tree hollows or on the ground.
FUN FACT: During breeding season, the male's head is washed with orange-yellow, and the knob on its bill increases in size.

Javan Tree Duck
(see The Oasis, page 17)

White-faced Whistling-Duck
(see The Oasis, page 16)

Eyton Tree Duck ❑ ▼
Dendrocygna eytoni
Grazing on grasses, herbs, grains, and seeds in the meadows and plains, and also near the lagoons and swamps of their native Australia, these plumed ducks prefer to make their home on land rather than in the water. Their reproductive cycle is largely dependent on the weather. During the rainy season, breeding numbers are far higher than during the dry season. Breeding is the only time this duck leaves its land-based home, building its nest near water; after the eggs are hatched, the ducklings are led to the water and supervised by both parents.
FUN FACT: Eyton Tree Ducks will travel up to 20 miles to find a satisfactory place to feed.

Marbled Teal ❑ ▲
Marmaronetta angustirostris
An endangered species, the Marbled Teal is the rarest duck in Europe. It appears large-headed because of its short, shaggy, hanging nape crest. These ducks are seasonal travelers, seeking other locations during the summer dry season in the Mediterranean basin. Always staying near the shore, in shallow freshwater pools and marshes, they feed by dabbling in shallow waters; their diet consists of tubers, aquatic plants and invertebrates, mollusks, and worms. Their nests are built near the water, lined with grass and down, and protected from view by vegetation.

Anthurium hookeri ☐ ▲
Bird's Nest Anthurium
Many members of the *Anthurium* genus are known for their colorful flowers, which are long-lasting when cut. They can be found in the mountain forests of the tropical Americas. The flowers of this particular variety, *A. hookeri*, although attractive, are not showy. The leaves are leathery and similar in shape to tobacco leaves. Look in the understory for this low-growing plant species.

Allamanda cathartica ☐ ▲
Golden Trumpet or Common Allamanda
Some of the well-known relatives of *Allamanda* are Vinca, Oleander, and Frangipani. Like its relatives, this plant has a milky sap. All are native to the tropical Americas. *A. cathartica* is the best-known member of its genus and grows as an espalier (a vine trained to grow in a particular pattern), sometimes reaching heights of up to 50 feet.

Cuphea llavea ☐ ◄
Bat-faced Cuphea
Native to Mexico, this shrub tends to stay rather small, usually growing to a height of no more than 18 inches. The blooms are purple and red. One variety of this plant has the name 'Tiny Mice' because its blooms resemble mouse ears.
FUN FACT: Bat-faced Cuphea is best known by the plant keepers at DISNEY'S ANIMAL KINGDOM® PARK as the Mickey Mouse plant.

Cyperus papyrus ☐ ▶
Egyptian Paper Reed
Cyperus papyrus, native to Africa, has been around for many millennia. Ancient Egyptians flattened and dried the stems of the plant to make a type of paper. This plant

looks perfect in a water garden. The unusual flower head, which resembles an umbrella of sorts, adds to the plant's distinctive appearance. *C. papyrus* is happiest when placed in a location where the roots will remain under 2 inches to 3 feet of water.

Gardenia jasminoides ❑ ◄
Jasmine Gardenia

Native to China and a member of the coffee family, *Gardenia jasminoides* was once called Cape Jasmine. It is considered one of the world's most fragrant flowers. In Hawaii, its sought-after blooms are used in some of the most expensive leis. The flowers of *G. jasminoides* are also used to make tea and can be eaten as a delicacy—raw or pickled or preserved in honey.

Jasminum nitidum ❑ ▲
Angel Wing Jasmine

The leaves of this shrub tend to be more oblong than round, giving them the appearance of "angel wings." Found native in Asia and Africa, this climber performs best when grown to cover an arch or a trellis.

FUN FACT: The flowers are so fragrant that some of the Jasminum *species are used to make jasmine perfume.*

Jatropha integerrima ❑ ▲
Peregrina or Spicy Jatropha

To locate this plant, look for its star-shaped, coral-red flowers. *Jatropha integerrima* has a milky white sap that appears when the plant stems or leaves are broken. Often it is difficult to use the leaves of *J. integerrima* for identification because they can be quite irregular. This shrub, which is indigenous to the West Indies and Peru, can reach heights of 20 feet; it makes an attractive addition to a butterfly garden.

Epipremnum aureum ❑ ▶
Golden Pothos

Pothos is a popular plant; it's easy to take care of and grows in shady conditions. *Epipremnum aureum,* native to Southeast Asia and the western Pacific, is a relative of pothos and just as easy to care for. However, it more closely resembles the Swiss Cheese Plant (*Monstera deliciosa*; see page 125). One characteristic of this genus is that the appearance of the leaf changes with the age of the plant. *E. aureum* lives on the floor of the rain forest in deep shade. In order to find sunlight it will travel over the ground, locate a large tree, send out aerial roots, and climb the tree. As the plant climbs, the leaves get larger the higher the plant goes. Regardless of the plant's age, the leaf size will not increase if the plant is not growing vertically. Don't be fooled when you look for this plant—check the leaves at the base of the tree and in the canopy for a positive ID.

Lagerstroemia indica ❏ ▲
Crape Myrtle

The Crape Myrtle, native to India, is one of the most popular flowering trees in the southern United States. The *Lagerstroemia speciosa*, or Queen's Crape Myrtle, is a close relative; the name *speciosa* means "showy," and the tree's pink-red blooms are just that. Many varieties of crape myrtle grow in DISNEY'S ANIMAL KINGDOM® PARK. Some were cultivated from seed that was collected from as far away as Bali and Thailand. In addition to the flowers, many of the varieties have colorful bark that is striking even after the leaves fall. These trees provide a show year-round, whether it's the blooms in the summer, the colorful leaves in the fall, or the colorful bark for the rest of the year.

Mussaenda spp. ❏ ▼

These plants, native to Asia, tropical Africa, and the Pacific Islands, have no common name. Plants in this family, Rubiaceae, mostly made up of climbers, can put on quite a show. They will bloom during the summer, and in many locations they bloom year-round. The flowers tend to be on the small side, but the plants'

Leonotis menthafolia
❏ ▲
Lion's Ear

One guess at what this bloom resembles? Another name is Lion's Tail. This interesting plant has flower stems that display a spiky, spidery, orange bloom about every 10 inches up the stem. The flower stems can reach heights up to 5 feet. *Leonotis menthafolia* is often grown in large containers to showcase its unusual blooms. The plant lives in southern Africa and tropical areas where it can receive full sun throughout the day.

showy color comes from the bracts. Bracts are modified leaves that surround the flower and are usually small and not very noticeable. In the case of *Mussaenda* species, however, one bract is enlarged and extremely colorful. The leaves and the sepals have a velvet-like appearance. This plant will produce yellow, pink, white, and red bracts. *Mussaenda* species do not like the cold, so if you plan to purchase one of your own, put it under cover when the temperature drops.

Mussaenda erythrophylla

Mussaenda philippica

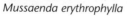

Nelumbo lutea ❏ ▲
American Lotus

The lotus most commonly seen in Southeast Asia is a water plant and is known for the stunning size of the leaves and flowers it produces: the leaves on some of the varieties reach 3 feet or more. There are many uses for the lotus beyond ornamentation. The flowers are very fragrant, and after they set seed, the seed heads are often used in dried arrangements. Cosmetics were once made with the pollen from the flowers. The plant is a versatile food source: the tubers are used in Chinese cooking and are high in vitamin C and protein; the starchy, under-ground rhizomes, when baked, are said to resemble sweet potatoes; the plant's half-ripe seeds are delicious, similar in flavor to chest-nuts. The lotus can grow in any waterway that does not freeze. If there is a danger of a freeze, it can be planted in tubs and moved into a holding area until the cold has passed. The plant is prominent in the Hindu and Buddhist religions, an important feature in offerings and works of art. Lotus seeds have been found in ancient Egyptian tombs and were depicted in hieroglyphics.

FUN FACT: Lotus seeds found in Japan—and shown by carbon dating to be 2,000 years old—have germinated and borne flowers.

Pyrostegia venusta ❏ ▶
Flame Vine

The English translation of *Pyrostegia venusta* is "fire on the roof." Native to South America, this brilliant crawler will reach heights of 30 feet or more in warmer areas. The plant is grown primarily for its gorgeous, abundant display of gold-orange flowers in the fall, winter, and spring.

Petrea volubilis ❏ ▲
Purple Queen's Wreath

The blue flowers of this vine-like plant are easy to spot in the tropical forest—blue is not a com-mon color for blooms. The flower clusters of this plant are similar to the lilac. The individual flowers have five petals and resemble a star. Native to South America and the West Indies, this plant can grow to a height of 30 feet or more, producing thick stems over time.

FUN FACT: The plant's Latin name honors Lady Petre, a patron of botanists and wife of a British administrator in colonial India.

Russelia equisetiformis □ ▲
Firecracker Plant

Native to Mexico, the Firecracker Plant has flowers that look like tiny, red firecrackers. It performs best in full sun and will reach heights of 4 to 5 feet; without regular hard pruning, it can get out of hand.

FUN FACT: When you first see it, you may wonder, "Without leaves, how does this plant produce its food?" The Russelia equisetiformis *uses the green surfaces of the stem for food production. The lack of leaves gives the plant the appearance of a grass, which it is not.*

Tecoma stans

Tecoma garrocha and Tecoma stans □ ◄
Trumpet Vine or Madam Golden and Yellow Elder

Tecoma garrocha and *T. stans* are native to Central and South America. The members of this genus are small evergreen shrubs and climbers, which makes them ideal for a trellis or an archway. The flowers of *T. garrocha* bear a slight resemblance to those found on a honeysuckle; the yellow flowers of *T. stans* inspired its common name, Yellow Elder. *T. garrocha* produces a long (6 to 8 inches) bean-pod-like fruit that is very narrow and thin.

Tecoma garrocha

44

AFRICA

Crossing the bridge over the Discovery River, you'll enter Harambe Village, an area fashioned after a 500-year-old East African coastal village. Plants here are adapted to a hot, dry environment with seasonal monsoons. Straight ahead is the queue for the KILIMANJARO SAFARIS® attraction, where you can see the Abyssinian Blue-winged Goose and the West African Crowned Crane.

KILIMANJARO SAFARIS®

From the time you stand in the queue for the KILIMANJARO SAFARIS attraction until you disembark the safari vehicle, you will ride through five habitats: Ituri Forest, Safi River, West Savanna, Savanna Flamingo Pool, and East Savanna.

West African Crowned Crane ❏ ▶

Balearica pavonina

In the area near The Tree of Life you may have seen the East African Crowned Crane. Here, in the queue for the KILIMANJARO SAFARIS, you can see its West African cousin. Actually, there is little difference between them. The neck of the West African is black and the neck of the East African is gray. Both are highly social; both pair off, usually for life; and both assume joint responsibility with their mates for their offspring.

Black Rhinoceros ❏ ▶

Diceros bicornis minor

In the Ituri Forest, you will see a Black Rhinoceros that is older than the two-year old in this photo. Just as the elephant has been poached for its tusks throughout its range, so has the rhinoceros been hunted for its horn. Local regulations and international conservation efforts are united in bringing back the populations that once roamed the African land. Massive and at times aggressive, the Black Rhinoceros (it's really gray) can weigh as much as 3,000 pounds and run at 35 miles per hour; its horns can reach 4 feet in length. Its triangular upper lip is used for grasping food from trees, much like an elephant's trunk. Left undisturbed, Black Rhinos are mostly sedentary, solitary creatures, content to browse on trees and shrubs, wallow in the mud to stay cool and keep off the flies—and sleep. *FUN FACTS: The horn of a rhino is made of compressed keratin, much like our fingernails. If the horn comes off, it will regenerate, especially in young animals.*

Abyssinian Blue-winged Goose ❑ ◄
Cyanochen cyanopterus

From the queue, you may see these distinctive-looking, pale, green-feathered geese. Native to the Ethiopian highlands, they are relatively sedentary, feeding on the grasses and plants (and sometimes worms, snails, and small reptiles) of their home turf. If this otherwise non-aggressive goose is upset, it will let you know with a high-pitched whistle.

Helmeted Guinea Fowl ❑ ►
Numida meleagris

The Helmeted is the most common species of guinea fowl. In its African homeland the Helmeted Guinea Fowl thrives on seeds, tubers, bulbs, and, when available, invertebrates. Its habitat and breeding ground are always close to water. Breeding usually occurs following the rainy season; the female will lay up to 12 eggs. If you happen to see 50 eggs in a single nest, you will know that more than one female has been making deposits.

FUN FACT: The history of the Helmeted Guinea Fowl can be traced to the 4th century BC, when they were prized for their meat and sometimes kept as pets.

Bongo ❑ ▲
Tragelaphus eurycerus

Of the forest antelopes, the Bongo is the largest and may be the most colorful: it is chestnut red with white torso stripes and a striking chevron between the eyes. What the Bongo lacks in speed it makes up for in its keen sense of hearing and its ability to jump great heights. Found mainly in the forests of eastern, central, and western Africa, Bongos travel solo, in pairs, or in small groups of females with their young and one male. Males can weigh as much as 600 pounds, females up to 540 pounds; newborns weigh in at an impressive 48-plus pounds.

FUN FACT: Both male and female Bongos have spiral, lyre-shaped horns that they use for defense.

Nyala ❑ ▶
Tragelaphus angasi

Making its home in the savannas of southeastern Africa, the Nyala is a large, agile member of the antelope family. There is a great difference in appearance between the male and the female. The male ranges in weight from 235 to 255 pounds, is shaggy gray with vertical white stripes, and has horns, a beard, a crest along the neck and back, and—unusual among antelopes—a black fringe that runs from withers to rump. The female is much smaller (150 to 175 pounds) and lighter in color: she has a pale chestnut coat, brighter white stripes than the male, a short black crest along the back, and no horns. The young—both male and female—resemble the adult female. A sociable species, Nyalas live in herds and feed on grass, leaves, flowers, and fruit.

FUN FACT: The Nyala makes a clicking sound both in courtship and to communicate with its young.

Yellow-backed Duiker ❏ ▶

Cephalophus sylvicultor
Appropriately named, this member of the antelope family has a highly visible yellow patch of hair on its rump, which becomes erect when the animal senses danger. The Yellow-backed is the largest (135 to 175 pounds) of the 17 species of duikers, but its arched body shape enables it to slip easily through foliage to hide. Solitary creatures that travel alone or in pairs, duikers are also elusive. They browse by night for their diet of berries and plants and spend the day sleeping in the undergrowth. Yellow-backed Duikers occasionally feed on small animals or insects, and they will at times stand up on their hind legs to feed on vegation that otherwise would be out of reach.

FUN FACT: The duiker's ability to hide or dive into the dense vegetation of the southern African forest explains its name: duiker *is Afrikaans for "diver."*

Okapi ❏ ▼

Okapia johnstoni
Although it looks like a relative of the zebras, the Okapi is actually a member of the giraffe family. It has white, zebra-like stripes on its lower rump and legs, which creates an excellent camouflage, and a long, supple neck that allows it to stretch high into the trees for food. The Okapi's home is only in the equatorial rain forests of the Democratic Republic of the Congo, where it feeds on shoots, forest plants, grasses, and ferns.

FUN FACTS: The Okapi has hoof glands, is relatively solitary, and communicates with scent and voice rather than with visual signals.

OKAPI

Like a giraffe, the Okapi has a sticky, blue-black tongue that is more than a foot long. The Okapi uses its tongue to reach up to high branches and snag edible leaves and berries. It is also an ideal grooming tool for its entire body, even long enough to reach the Okapi's ears and clean its eyes.

Pink-backed Pelican ❑ ▲
Pelecanus rufescens

This pink-backed bird can have gray, yellow, or red legs. At their most colorful during breeding season, the pelican's bare parts then fade until the next breeding period. Living in freshwater lakes, swamps, and rivers, the pelican prefers to nest in trees near its waterfront home. Two eggs are laid in a stick nest; chicks are naked when hatched, and sibling rivalry is rampant in this species. The result? There's a high mortality rate among newborns.

FUN FACT: The pelican's large bill has a greater capacity for food than its stomach.

CORMORANTS

The cormorant is a skilled fishing bird and is highly valued for its abilities. In a tradition dating back 1,000 years, river fisherman in southern China have learned to harness the cormorant's fishing prowess. Although the birds catch the fish with their bills, a thin length of twine secured around their necks prevents them from swallowing the fish. A single fisherman on a bamboo raft can catch 40 pounds of fish a day with four trained birds.

Stanley Crane or Blue Crane ❑ ▲
Anthropoides paradisea

The Stanley Crane is one of only two crane species that have a completely feathered head. During the winter, when cranes are not breeding, they gather in flocks of up to 300 birds, many often engaging in competition for dominance over another member of the group; most of the time it is the males who engage in these chases, but occasionally females have been known to enter combat as well. Found in the grasslands and wetlands of southern and southeastern Africa, the Stanley Crane feeds on seeds, roots, locusts, grasshoppers, worms, reptiles, and small mammals.

FUN FACT: The Stanley Crane is the national bird of the Republic of South Africa.

Yellow-billed Stork ❏ ◀
Mycteria ibis
Aside from enhancing this red-faced stork's appearance, its deep yellow bill serves an important purpose: frogs, small fish, and aquatic insects are quickly consumed when the bird opens this bill—and then snaps it shut. Yellow-billed Storks feed only during brief periods of the day; the rest of the time they wade and socialize in shallow water. When breeding, they often nest with other storks. The young are born completely helpless, and both male and female care for them until they're able to manage on their own—usually in about three months.

Saddle-billed Stork
(see The Tree of Life, page 37)

White-breasted Cormorant ❏ ▼
Phalacrocorax lucidus
Crossing over the Safi River, you will pass the White-breasted Cormorant. These very social birds travel in large numbers in eastern Africa, even when breeding. The courtship ritual—and, later, the bonding with their young—is noteworthy: a wooing male waves its wings, opening and closing them in a sweeping motion; when he has attracted the female, both birds entwine their necks and preen each other. It is the male that gathers materials for the nest—usually sticks, branches, seaweed, and feathers—and brings them to the female, who actually builds the nesting place. Both male and female participate in incubating the eggs, usually for a period of 28 days.

Nile Crocodile ❑ ▲
Crocodylus niloticus

Along the Safi River you will see the Nile Crocodile, the largest species of crocodile in Africa (if not the world), which weighs upward of 1,500 pounds, can measure over 20 feet in length, and has very sharp teeth and a powerful lower jaw that can grip tightly. Living in and around rivers, lakes, and swamps, this animal subsists on mammals, birds, fish, carrion—and other crocodiles. Cold-blooded creatures, crocodiles regulate their body temperature by controlling their exposure to the elements of their environment: they sunbathe only in the cooler part of the day, spending the hottest times lolling under a tree.

FUN FACT: The eyes, nostrils, and ears of the crocodile lie along the top of its head so that it can see, hear, smell, and breathe when its body is submerged in water.

Nile Hippopotamus ❑ ◀
Hippopotamus amphibious

The Nile Hippopotamus is enormous: adults weigh between 2,500 and 4,500 pounds, and even a newborn weighs in at a hefty 80 to 110 pounds. Hippos are well adapted for their primarily water-based existence: eyes, nostrils, and ears are set high on the head, allowing for long periods of immersion. In fact, when threatened, a hippo can remain totally underwater for up to 12 minutes. Nile Hippos come out of the water at night, often covering as much as 20 miles on land in search of food (grasses, water plants, leaves, and bark).

FUN FACTS: The Nile Hippos have produced several offspring that you may see swimming in the Safi River alongside the females. Calves are born in the water, nurse underwater, and swim before they can walk.

NILE HIPPOPOTAMUS
Appearing almost hairless, the copper to dark brown Nile Hippopotamus has glandular skin that oozes red droplets, probably the origin of the phrase "sweating blood."

Northern Pintail ❑ ▼
Anas acuta

The Northern Pintail is named for its two long, central feathers, found only on the male (drake). These ducks have black-and-white underparts, a white neck, and a brown face and crown. Females are a plain, mottled brownish white. Both sexes have long, graceful necks—well suited for peering over high grasses and feeding in deep water. Found in areas as far-reaching as Canada, the United States (including Hawaii), western Africa, and Asia, the Northern Pintail is an accomplished flier, usually soaring in V-formation. A 6,000-mile migration to their winter homes in Hawaii is not uncommon.

Yellow-billed Duck ❑ ▼
Anas undulata

The most colorful parts of these ducks are their bright green wing-patches and the bright yellow bill that gives them their name. Making their home in the rivers, lakes, and open waters of Africa, these birds gather in large numbers during the dry season and travel great distances during the rainy season.

Egyptian Goose ❑ ▼

Alopochen aegyptiacus

The Egyptian Goose is a member of the distinctive sheldgeese family. In the water, it swims with its rear end held higher than its shoulders. It is among the most aggressive species of waterfowl, especially during the breeding season. The Egyptian Goose has reddish-orange plumage, pale cinnamon breast and underparts, and a distinctive facial pattern. The birds build their nests in the old nests of other species, either

in the ground, in holes, or in trees. An average-size flock of 100 Egyptian Geese (flock size can be as large as a thousand) can destroy a crop field in short order.

FUN FACT: Students of antiquity know that the ancient Egyptians considered the Egyptian Goose sacred and depicted it on many of their monuments.

Mandrill ❑ ▲

Mandrillus sphinx

Moving into the West Savanna, you may catch a glimpse of the Mandrill, which is among the largest of the terrestrial (ground-dwelling, as opposed to tree-dwelling) baboons. Though it may appear ferocious—especially the male, which has bright purple, blue, and scarlet coloring on its face and rear end—the Mandrill is a non-aggressive, highly social creature. At home in the rain forests of western and central Africa, Mandrills live in groups of up to 400 individuals, with at least one adult male and several females and their young. Most of the Mandrill's day is spent on its primary activity: foraging for fruits, leaves, insects, and eggs; this animal can cover as much as 20 square miles in a day as it looks for food.

FUN FACT: Unlike most other members of the animal kingdom (except humans), when the Mandrill bares its teeth it is a greeting, not a threat.

White Pelican ❑ ▲
Pelecanus onocrotalus
The one sure way to spot a
White Pelican in breeding
condition is to look at its
face: the male "blushes" a
pinkish yellow and the
female a bright orange;
the legs of both sexes
turn crimson (at non-
breeding times these birds
have pale pink legs and
black feathers). Due to
its voracious appetite
(primarily for fish), the
White Pelican needs
to eat numerous times
every day.
*FUN FACTS: The long,
sieve-like bill of the pelican
can hold up to 3.5 gallons at
a time. Once the bill is filled
to capacity, it filters out the
water and saves the fish.*

White-faced Whistling-Duck
(see The Oasis, page 16)

MANDRILLS
*Mandrills are difficult to observe
in the wild, and much remains to
be learned about their behavior.
All Mandrills, for example, have
a scent gland in their chests.
They deposit the scent this
gland exudes by embracing a
tree and rubbing their chests
against the trunk. But it's not
clear whether this is done to
mark territory or simply as a
means of communicating with
other roaming Mandrills.*

Grant's Zebra ❑ ▲
Equus burchelli bohmi

In the West Savanna, the safari vehicle passes the white-and-black-striped zebras, which make their home in the savannas, grass steppes, hills, and mountains of eastern Africa. The social structure is a one-male harem system. When male zebras mature, they break away from the family they were born into and form groups of young bachelors. Families' territories (which can span up to 124 square miles) are usually shared, with individuals taking turns as lookouts for predators. When threatened, the family closes up and takes flight. Zebras spend much of their time grazing on grass, leaves, and bark and settle in areas near water. Mature males weigh 775 to 850 pounds, females 700 to 750. Foals, which weigh 70 pounds at birth, can stand almost immediately and run within an hour, but they are not weaned until seven to ten months old.

FUN FACT: No two zebras have precisely the same striping pattern. Although they may seem conspicuous to us, in fact their stripes provide great camouflage in the high grasses.

Patterson's Eland ❑ ▶
Taurotragus oryx

Natives of the grasslands and open woodlands of eastern, southern, and central Africa, elands feed on grass and the foliage of trees and bushes, and can go for a month without water, getting liquid from melons and thick-leafed plants. A higher-than-normal body temperature allows the eland to survive in the desert. Traveling in herds of 25 to 70, elands are often led by two adult males (bulls). They grunt when grazing and give a soft call, or mew, to their calves but will bellow when they sense danger. With the tendons of their forelegs, mature bulls produce a clicking sound that can be heard at great distances.

FUN FACT: In open areas, elands can be seen high-jumping and broad-jumping over one another from almost a standing start.

Impala ❑ ▲
Aepyceros melampus
The most agile and
most numerous mem-
ber of the antelope
family, the Impala is
common prey for lions, leopards, and cheetahs.
This animal's greatest defense is its ability to run
40 miles per hour, jump 10 feet in the air (and
turn in mid-air), and leap a distance of 30 feet.
Impalas live in herds of up to 100, mainly as a
means of protection: if a predator attacks, the
herd scatters, leaping and running in all direc-
tions. Found in the open woodlands, sand bush
country, and acacia savannas of southern and
eastern Africa, Impalas feed according to the
season, grazing on grass or browsing on foliage,
herbs, and shoots when grass is unavailable.

*FUN FACTS: Impalas have scent glands on their hind
legs below the hock (the joint midway up the leg)
that are used to mark territories. The scent from these
glands is dispersed in the air as the animals leap and
may confuse a predator.*

Reticulated Giraffe ❑ ▲
Giraffa camelopardalis
The statistics speak for themselves: the giraffe is the world's tallest animal, measuring up to 20 feet in height; it can weigh as much as 2,500 pounds; its neck can measure 6 feet; its tail—including the tuft at the end—also reaches a length of 6 feet; its 18-inch tongue can sweep the leaves from a tree branch in one lick; it has a stride of 15 feet (giraffes are pacers, they swing both legs on one side of the body at one time, then the other side); it can run at a speed of 45 miles per hour; and even a newborn calf is 6 feet tall and weighs in at an impressive 125 to 150 pounds. Adult giraffes use their enormous front feet (9 x 12 inches) for defense against predators, such as lions and hyenas.

FUN FACT: Giraffes' large eyes afford them great vision. They are able to distinguish colors and see clearly over great distances.

GIRAFFES
Despite its length and flexibility, the neck of a giraffe is too short to reach the ground. In order to drink, the animal must awkwardly spread its legs wide so its head can reach the water. Not surprisingly, this position makes giraffes most vulnerable to predators. Their excellent eyesight enables them to quickly check out the terrain before drinking.

Sable Antelope ❑ ▶

Hippotragus niger

Among the handsomest members of the antelope family, the Sable makes its home in the savanna woodlands and grasslands of eastern and southern Africa. Both males (bulls) and females (cows) have pointed, ringed (or annulated) horns, a glossy black coat, and white facial markings. Sable Antelopes are large animals: adult males weigh up to 520 pounds, females 485 pounds. For food, they graze on the grasses, foliage, and herbs of their native habitat. This species is highly social, traveling in herds of 10 to 20 cows and their calves; during mating season, the bull establishes a separate breeding area and, when necessary, will fight other bulls to protect it.

FUN FACTS: When they sense danger, Sable Antelopes can run at speeds of up to 35 miles an hour. When fighting, they drop to their knees to engage their foes with their sizable horns.

White-bearded Wildebeest ❑ ▲

Connochaetes taurinus

What is it? With its cow-like horns, ox-like head, brown bands on its neck and shoulders, and white beard, it's hard to tell that this is actually a member of the antelope family. Populating the bush savannas and woodland areas of Africa, wildebeests travel in large herds; during migrations, tens of thousands can be found in one place. When calving, females enjoy the company of others; at such locations—either within a herd or at a migratory site—dozens of offspring can be produced in a single morning.

Thomson's Gazelle ❏ ▲
Gazella thomsoni

Easily identified in the savanna of DISNEY'S ANIMAL KINGDOM® PARK by its racing stripes, the Thomson's Gazelle can sprint at speeds of 50 miles per hour. Among the most graceful members of the antelope family, "Tommies" not only run fast, they can bound (or stot) into the air while running. This action is a diversionary tactic designed to confuse the gazelle's many predators and also gives it a clear view of what lies ahead. The most prominent feature of the male is its thick, ringed horns, which rise to 1.5 feet (a female's horns are thinner). The Thomson sweeps its black tail over its white rump to communicate at some distance. It is the favorite prey of the Cheetah.

FUN FACT: Territorial males regularly mark their boundaries with the scent of urine, dung, and scent glands, and they can be very aggressive in protecting these areas.

Secretary Bird ❏ ▶
Sagittarius serpentarius

The Secretary Bird is in a class by itself. Unlike other raptors, this bird has long legs, wings, and tail. The plumage is ash gray, except on the upper legs and the rear part of the back, which are black.

Groups of Secretary Birds move rapidly over the the ground on their long legs or fly like swans, with neck outstretched and legs extended, over the plains and grasslands of southern Africa. During the breeding season, male and female birds work together to build the nest, which is generally placed low in the fork of a tree.

FUN FACTS: Like many birds of prey, the Secretary Bird feeds on snakes. Using one of its wings as a shield against counterattack, it batters the reptile with its feet and, when necessary, jumps out of reach of a venomous bite with incredible speed.

Cape Teal ❑ ▶

Anas capensis

As the safari vehicle drives around the Savanna Flamingo Pool, you can get a scenic view of the Greater Flamingos (see page 33) and the Cape Teal. The waters of southeastern Africa—especially shallow lagoons, rivers, and coastal waters—are home to these greenish-gray ducks whose upturned bills seem almost white. Foraging during the day for the seeds, leaves, and stems ·of aquatic plants, they are excellent divers and can remain submerged for five seconds or more with their wings closed tightly. Though it is a favorite sporting bird, the Cape Teal is in no immediate danger of extinction.

FUN FACT: During mating, the male turns the back of his head toward the interested female, instead of facing her.

African Elephant ❑ ▼

Loxodonta africana

From the Savanna Flamingo Pool, the safari vehicle enters the East Savanna. Off on the left you will see the largest of the land animals, the African Elephants. They are also among the most gentle, intelligent, and social land animals. With adult males weighing in at 11,000 pounds (6,500 to 8,500 pounds for females), these citizens of the wild have enormous ears, which serve as fans to cool their bodies, and tusks that are actually teeth. Their trunks serve various functions: breathing, smelling, picking up food, drinking, bathing, swinging at threatening animals—and even investigating companions. Elephants are herbivores; their voracious appetites (their daily intake can equal 4 to 6 percent of their body weight) are well satisfied in their natural habitat.

FUN FACT: At birth, an African Elephant weighs between 150 and 350 pounds.

male

Cheetah ❏ ▲
Acinonyx jubatus

The Cheetah is designed like a sleek sports car. It is the fastest of all land mammals—lightly built, with long, slender legs, a long tail to ensure good balance, and unsheathed claws, designed for traction, that are especially useful when making a quick turn. Able to go from zero to 70 miles per hour in just three seconds, the Cheetah doesn't have the endurance of an automobile: it runs out of steam after about a quarter of a mile. The Cheetah stalks its prey (usually antelopes, hares, and rodents) and, when it is close, sets out on a short, high-speed chase. If its quarry outruns the Cheetah, the cat must recuperate from the exertion of the sprint before venturing out again in pursuit of other prey.

FUN FACT: History records that humans trained Cheetahs for hunting as early as 3000 BC.

African Lion ❑◀▶
Panthera leo

The largest of the African carnivores, these "kings of the jungle" are at home in the African grasslands and live in family groups (prides) of between 3 and 30. Although males dominate this society, the female is the principal hunter. Wildebeests and zebras are favorite prey. Lionesses have cubs approximately every two years and are fiercely protective of their young. Cubs begin to hunt small prey at 15 months, and although young females often remain with the pride, male cubs are forced out of the family by the dominant male.

FUN FACT: The lion may be fierce, but it is not fast. Hiding in the grasses, the lion is most successful stalking until it is close enough to ambush its prey.

female

Greater Kudu ❑ ▼
Tragelaphus strepsiceros

The Greater Kudu's biggest claims to fame are its stately, 5-foot-long, spiral horns (males only), the longest of any antelope. Used to inter-lock in play or in combat, the horns do not reach their full size of 2.5 turns until the Greater Kudu is six years old. The kudu's unusually large, cupped ears and bushy fringe of hair, which extends from the chin down the neck, are further distinguishing characteristics. The Greater Kudu is gregarious, forms lasting social bonds with females, and is non-territorial. Found in eastern, central, and southern Africa, the kudu subsists mainly on leaves and grass.

FUN FACT: Greater Kudus are terrific jumpers—even an 8-foot fence isn't too high for them.

Ostrich ❏ ◀
Struthio camelus

Despite its ungainly appearance, the Ostrich holds the distinction of being the world's largest bird; it runs faster than any other two-legged animal and lays the largest eggs of any living creature. At 6 to 7 feet tall and weighing up to 350 pounds, this fleet-footed, non-flying bird is native to parts of Africa, and can adapt to a variety of environments, from savanna grasslands to semi-deserts. At mating season, females lay as many as 12 eggs. The Ostrich's tall neck, keen eyesight, strong leg muscles, and two-toed, hoof-like feet (it can sprint at an amazing 45 miles per hour) allow it to escape predators.

FUN FACT: Like humans, the Ostrich has long eyelashes, mainly to keep dust from getting into its eyes.

Mhorr Gazelle ❏ ▶
Gazella dama mhorr

Now extinct in the wild, this gazelle is distinguished by its white face and chestnut-brown neck, shoulders, and back (other gazelles do not have coloring on their backs). Weighing up to 160 pounds, with short (16-inch) horns, the Mhorr Gazelle browses on woody plants, grasses, and herbs. When gazelles sense danger, they bound with all four legs leaving the ground at once, a gait called stotting. Males are extremely territorial (marking boundaries with urine and dung) and will engage in pushing and horn fighting; while fights can result in injuries, territorial battles are rarely fought to the death.

FUN FACT: The Mhorr is the largest member of the gazelle family.

STOTTING

Stotting is a stiff-legged jump or leap in which all four legs leave and return to the ground at the same time. The Thomson's Gazelle and the Mhorr Gazelle stot when they are playing but also when they are alarmed. Since a stotting gazelle can reach heights of 10 feet, it can view its course of retreat and alert other gazelles at the same time.

Ruppell's Griffon Vulture ❏ ▶
Gyps rueppelli

The Ruppell's Griffon is one of the largest vultures, with a wingspan of more than 8 feet. It scavenges for carrion in the arid steppes and grasslands of central Africa, and in cliffs and gorges when breeding. These vultures have a distinctive scaled feather pattern, yellow eyes, and an orange bill. Both male and female prepare the nest, on a platform of sticks or in a tree. The female lays a single, large white egg, and both share in its long (50-day) incubation and fledgling period.

FUN FACT: Ruppell's Griffon Vultures are social birds at carcasses. Several of them may gather around the carrion and fight over food, but there is an apparent social structure among them that determines who gets priority.

Scimitar-horned Oryx ❏ ▲
Oryx gazella dammah

Appropriately named for its lance-like, ridged horns, this oryx is built like a polo pony, with its level back, short neck, deep chest, and long limbs. Oryx are nomadic creatures and will travel great distances in search of food, usually grasses, roots, and bulbs. Once well adapted to their desert home (Egypt and Sudan), they were able to exist without water far longer than other large mammals, but now they are thought to be extinct in the wild. Despite its rather benign appearance, the Scimitar-horned Oryx is a highly aggressive animal; females are protective of their young and can be especially aggressive when they have a calf at their side.

FUN FACT: Scimitar-horned Oryxs develop digging skills from an early age. They dig a slight depression in the ground in which they lie down to rest.

Vulturine Guinea Fowl ❏ ◀

Acryllium vulturinum

These striking black-and-white-striped and cobalt-blue-spotted birds spend much of their time on the ground, and it would seem hard for them to camouflage themselves amid the bush. They are accustomed to their tropical home in the grasslands and plateaus of Africa and are able to go without water for long periods of time (even when water is available, they often do not drink). Though the Vulturine Guinea Fowl can fly, it prefers to run from danger—its long legs are a definite attribute.

FUN FACT: The Vulturine Guinea Fowl is the largest and most ornamented of the guinea fowl species.

Helmeted Guinea Fowl
(see page 47)

GUINEA FOWL

These active, ground-walking birds live in large groups in forest clearings and savannas and are always noisy. They scatter at the slightest alarm, coming together later when called by one of the older birds. During breeding season, they break up into pairs and later rejoin the group.

Waterbuck ❏ ▶

Kobus ellipsiprymnus

Although the Waterbuck weighs in at an impressive 550 pounds and has 3-foot-long annulated (ringed) horns, its best weapon against predators is the foul smell it emanates. Grazing on the grasses of its native African savanna, the Waterbuck—true to its name—needs lots of water to aid in its digestion. These creatures are social, living in small herds of up to 25 members—generally females and young and one dominant male. Only males have horns; they are highly territorial and will lock horns with any creature trying to encroach on their land. Females, however, are more willing to share.

FUN FACT: The Waterbuck's skin glands exude an oily secretion that makes its coat water-repellent.

White Rhinoceros ❑ ▲
Ceratotherium simum simum
Weighing in at up to 4,000 to 4,500 pounds, this rhinoceros should be able to ward off any would-be predators, and it can   except for humans, who have hunted it into near extinction. With no outside intervention, White Rhinos can live to their late 30s. Unlike the Black Rhino, the White is sociable, remaining close to water, which it drinks in large amounts (but can also go two days without). The White Rhino feeds mainly on the grasses of the African savanna, using its wide, square lips to "mow" up the short grass. Rhinos have poor vision; fortunately, their sense of hearing and smell more than compensate.
FUN FACT: The White Rhinoceros is not white at all but slate gray to yellow brown. The name derives from wijt, *which means "wide" in Afrikaans. Look at its mouth and you'll understand why.*

Warthog ❑ ▶
Phacochoerus aethiopicus
Resembling no other animal in the world, the Warthog may not be the most beautiful of nature's creatures, but it is coura-geous, loyal, and fiercely protective of its family. The Warthog has four tusks—the two more visible and longer ones (about 12 inch-es) are impressive; the lower, shorter, and less prominent two are used in

combat. This animal also digs for roots with its tusks. At home in the grasslands of Africa, Warthogs live as a family group (or sounder), seeking shelter in burrows.
FUN FACT: The warts, which are prominent only on the male (boar), are skin growths and have no bony support. They serve to cushion blows during battle.

PANGANI FOREST EXPLORATION TRAIL®

After exiting the safari, you can continue your adventure through Africa by taking the Pangani Forest Exploration Trail on your right. Walking down the trail, you will go through a research station, where you will see the Naked Mole Rat, African Bullfrog, Baboon Spider, and Euromastyx, and learn about the unusual behaviors of these small creatures. Continue on the path to the Aviary, the Underwater Viewing Area, the Savanna Overlook, and Gorilla Falls.

AFRICA AVIARY

DISNEY'S ANIMAL KINGDOM® PARK has brought into its aviary a variety of birds. Some are common; some are rare; some are easier to spot than others. Some are extremely vocal, while others are virtually silent. Spend some time here and see if you can spot all of them, even the ones not pictured here.

Of the aquatic birds, look for the African Pygmy Goose, the Hottentot Teal, the African Jacana, the White-backed Duck, and the Black Crake.

The African Grey Parrot is the only member of the Psittaciformes (see page 12) in the area. And the Olive Pigeon (not shown here) is the only member of the dove family. The Hadada Ibis, like all other ibises, has a down-curved bill that is used for pulling food out of the mud and soil. The Hammerkop, another sizable bird, builds one of the world's largest, most intricately formed nests.

The aviary's colorful perching birds include the black-and-red Bearded Barbet, the insect-eating Carmine Bee-eater, four species of starlings—the Amethyst, Emerald, Gold-breasted, and Superb—and the highly territorial Racquet-tailed Roller.

Two species of turacos—the Lady Ross's and the White-bellied Go-Away—are exotic birds worth seeking out. The feathers of the Lady Ross's Turaco differ from those of other birds in that they contain real color that can be extracted from the feather. The color substance, called turacin, has been used for research on leukemia.

And don't overlook the small but colorful Taveta Golden Weaver, the Snowy-headed Robin Chat, and the Magpie Shrike.

Hadada
Ibis ❑ ▲
Bostrychia hagedash

African Pygmy
Goose ❑ ◄
Nettapus auritus

Black Crake ❑ ▲
Amaurornis flavirostris

African Grey Parrot ❑ ▲
Psittacus erithacus

Hottentot
Teal ❑ ►
Anas punctata

STARLINGS

Unlike many Asian and European starling species, the African starlings featured in DISNEY'S ANIMAL KINGDOM® PARK are celebrated for their spectacular, iridescent coloring. The violet Amethyst Starling can appear blue or crimson, depending upon the light. The Emerald Starling is a shimmering mix of green and violet. The Superb Starling is a spectacular cross of bright orange and blue-black. The Golden-breasted Starling—with its green head, blue cheeks, blue wings, and purple and golden-yellow breast—is one of the most dazzling starlings.

Amethyst Starling ❑ ▲
Cinnyricinclus leucogaster

Superb Starling ❑ ▲
Spreo superbus

Emerald Starling ❑ ▲
Lamprotornis iris

Golden-breasted Starling ❑ ▲
Cosmopsarus regius

Racquet-tailed Roller ❑ ▲
Coracias spatulata

White-backed Duck ❑ ▲
Thalassornis leuconotus leuconotus

White-bellied Go-away Turaco ❑ ▼
Criniferoides leucogaster

Lady Ross's Turaco ❑ ▲
Musophaga rossae

African Jacana ❑ ▲
Actophilornis africana

Taveta Golden Weaver
❑ ▶
Ploceus castaneiceps

Bearded Barbet ❑ ▲
Lybius dubius

Hammerkop Stork ❑ ▲
Scopus umbretta

71

Nile Hippopotamus ❑ ▲

Hippopotamus amphibious

When you leave the Aviary, continue to walk on the trail to the underwater viewing area, where you will have a bottom's-up view of the Nile Hippo (see pages 52–53 for more information). Exit the underwater viewing area and continue on to the Savanna Overlook.

Abyssinian Ground Hornbill ❑ ▲

Bucorvus abyssinicus

Although they are birds, these hornbills do not fly often. They are cumbersome, almost clumsy, in flight and are more comfortable walking on tiptoe through their African savanna home. The size of a turkey, the Abyssinian Ground Hornbill has a long black bill that is handy for grasping objects, such as the small animals that make up its diet. The birds have an inflatable red foreneck, with a blue area at the front of the throat, and the skin on their throat and face is unfeathered.

Gerenuk ❑ ▲
Litocranius walleri

Because of its long, slender neck (which is only 7 to 10 inches in circumference), the Gerenuk is often called the "Giraffe Gazelle." Its horns (on males only) are massive, heavily ridged, and curve backward and then hook forward at the tip. Sedentary animals, Gerenuks spend about 65 percent of their day eating—like most African animals, Gerenuks require little to no water—and the rest of their time sleeping or strolling around their territory (which they mark by urinating and defecating). When it senses danger, the Gerenuk will stand motionless behind a bush until the threat has passed.

FUN FACTS: The trademark of the Gerenuk is its ability to stand upright on its powerful hind legs, unsupported. Its pointed tongue and flexible lips penetrate often thorny bushes to eat the leaflets.

Gunther's Dik-Dik ❑ ▲
Madoqua guentheri
Gunther's Dik-Dik is a shy creature that prefers the low thicket vegetation and brush of its native Africa. Research suggests that the dik-dik absorbs most of its water from the plants it eats and its kidneys are adapted to retain this fluid economically. If threatened, dik-diks dash away in zigzag leaps, but their small size (about 13 pounds) and unimpressive running ability make them vulnerable to predators.
FUN FACT: The name dik-dik is derived from the "zik-zik" sound the animals produce when excited.

Marabou Stork ❑ ▲
Leptoptilos crumeniferus
Except for a few bristles, the head of the Marabou Stork is bald, and a pouch hangs from its featherless neck. Don't be misled by seeing the Marabou spread its wings to shade fish from the steamy, tropical sun. Once the unsuspecting fish swims into the cooling shade, it is stabbed by the stork's sharp bill. Although ungainly in appearance, the Marabou Stork is a strong flyer, soaring high like a vulture. In fact, these birds are often seen with vultures, scavenging for carrion.

Kori Bustard ❑ ▲
Ardeotis kori
Bustards are running birds. They have heavy bodies and fly clumsily but are able to run with great speed. Bustards are closely related to cranes but have a shorter neck and larger body and tail. The Kori (or Giant) is the largest of the bustards, measuring 4.5 feet long. These elusive creatures make their home in the open grasslands and wooded savannas of Africa; little is known about their behavior, breeding habits, or lifespan. What is known is that their migration is based on the availability of water and food (insects, reptiles, and small rodents).

GORILLAS
Gorillas walk on their knuckles, which produces calluses on the back of their hands and preserves the sensitivity of their dexterous fingers.

Slender-tailed Meerkat ❏ ▷

Suricata suricatta

Proving that size isn't everything (an adult male weighs only up to 35 ounces), these enterprising creatures gain strength from their community, banding in large numbers to discourage predators many times their size. Often sharing their burrow with ground squirrels, Red Meerkats, and Yellow Mongooses, Slender-tailed Meerkats live in male-dominated, highly organized packs of up to 30 members and feed on butterflies, termites, crickets, spiders, scorpions, insects, eggs, and fruit—in other words, just about anything they can obtain.

FUN FACT: Communicating through chatter and barks, meerkats share duties: sentries secure the area, babysitters tend to the young, and other groups search for food.

Western Lowland Gorilla ❏ ▽

Gorilla gorilla gorilla

The PANGANI FOREST EXPLORATION TRAIL® adventure ends with the gorilla habitat. Found in the tropical rain forest of west-central Africa, these largest and most powerful of all primates are also among the least aggressive (their chest-beating is performed as a display). Weighing in at from 250 (females) to 600 pounds (adult males, called silverbacks), standing 5 to 6 feet tall, and with powerful arms stretching 7 to 8 feet, gorillas could easily intimidate. But watching them within their troop (sometimes up to 30 members), one sees families coexisting, building nests on the ground, grooming each other, feeding on bamboo shoots, fruit, and plants found on the forest floor, and engaging in playful wrestling with younger members.

Agave americana □ ▶
Century Plant

This plant's common name is somewhat of a misnomer, as it is unlikely to take 100 years to flower, but it does often need between 12 and 20 years to bloom. The flower stalk is impressive, able to grow up to 5 inches in one day and reaching heights of 20 feet, with the upper third of the stalk branching into the shape of a candelabra. The flowers will remain on the plant for months; after the bloom fades, the flower stalk dies. This plant, native to Mexico, works well as an ornamental.

FUN FACTS: The fibers of plants in this genus are used to produce sisal. Sap from the flower stem is sweet and can be distilled to produce tequila. Members of the Kickapoo tribe bake the tender, asparagus-like flower stems on hot stones, creating a food called quiote.

Beaucarnea stricta □ ▲
Ponytail Palm

Native to Mexico and the southwestern United States, the Ponytail Palm can take up to 10 years to flower. Related to yuccas, this tree has a thick-bottomed trunk. Older specimens can achieve massive dimensions, with a swollen base as much as 12 feet wide, supporting multiple trunks that can grow as tall as 15 feet.

Brugmansia hybrid □ ▲
Angel's Trumpet

In this genus, native to South America, some species can reach heights of 30 feet or more. The flowers are followed by large seed capsules. The fact that the large exotic flowers face downward has inspired a variety of common names in many languages, including Ground-gazing Flower.

Calotropis gigantea ❑ ▶
Crown Flower

The Crown Flower thrives in dry areas that are exposed to ocean winds and grows wild along the coastlines of Southeast Asia and the Pacific Islands. A member of the milkweed family, this large, sprawling shrub has oval, light-green leaves, milky stems, and continuous clusters of waxy, lavender, or white flowers; each flower consists of five pointed petals in a star shape, from the center of which rises a small "crown."

FUN FACTS: The long-lasting Crown Flower is used widely in Southeast Asia and the Pacific Islands in floral arrangements and as a decorative element. The flowers have been depicted in carved ivory, were regarded as emblems of royalty by Hawaii's Queen Liluokalani, and are used in sacred rituals in some parts of Bali.

Cordia sebestena ❑ ◀
Geiger Tree

The Geiger Tree is native to Florida, the West Indies, and Venezuela. Some trees in this genus are used for timber, and others are made into canoes; the leaves of *Cordias* have also been used to make dyes. The bright red-orange flowers are followed by fruit that can be eaten raw or boiled and pickled.

FUN FACT: The Geiger Beetle makes its home in this tree.

Eriobotrya japonica ❑ ▲
Loquat

Eriobotrya japonica is widely grown all over the world. It blooms in spring with creamy white, fragrant flowers, which develop into delicious fruit by summer and fall.

FUN FACTS: Fruit from the Loquat is eaten raw or stewed, cooked in sauces, preserved in jellies, and made into drinks. Loquat pie is made from fruit that is not fully ripe and is said to taste like cherry pie.

Kalanchoe beharensis ❑ ▲
Felt Bush

Pronounced with four syllables (KAL-an-ko-ee), this plant is native to Madagascar. Like most succulents, the members of this genus have fleshy, leathery leaves. Often these leaves have an unusual shape or appearance.

FUN FACTS: Of all the Kalanchoes, K. blossfeldiana is the most recognizable, and it is often associated with the December holiday season. K. blossfeldiana flowers according to the length of the day.

Morus alba 'Contorta' □ ▲
Contorted Mulberry

This small tree in the *Morus* genus is native to China. The variety 'Contorta' is cultivated for its unusual form. It grows in a twisted fashion, which gives the tree branches the appearance of being wrapped around a corkscrew. The edible fruit of many of the varieties is used to make wine or jam.

FUN FACT: An important reason for growing Morus alba *'Contorta' is to feed the silkworms that are used in the silk production industry.*

Pachypodium lamerei □ ▲

This unfriendly-looking plant is covered with inch-long spines. Because its appearance is unusual, *Pachypodium lamerei* makes a wonderful specimen plant for the "right spot."

VINES

The way vines grow is intriguing. Vining plants do not need to use all their energy for building hefty stems and trunks. Instead, they may trail over the ground, or climb on trees, other plants, rocks, or man-made structures. Vines climb in four ways:

- *Some climb by grasping the support with sticky rootlets.*
- *Some climb by twining their stems.*
- *Some use trendrils that attach to the support.*
- *Some vines have thorns that allow them to attach to a support and to climb over another plant.*

Not all vines climb upward. Some creep along the ground.

Podranea ricasoliana □ ▲
Pink Trumpet Vine

A southern African genus of only two species of twining vines, *Podranea* species are fast-growing plants that can grow up to 20 or 30 feet. Although there are many attractive climbers in DISNEY'S ANIMAL KINGDOM® PARK, only a few are as beautiful as the Pink Trumpet Vine.

Pachystachys lutea □ ▲
Golden Candles

Native to Peru, this small shrub got its common name because of its bright yellow bracts (modified leaves). When the bracts are fully spread, white flowers appear.

Ravenala madagascariensis ❑ ▲
Travelers Palm

This plant is very unusual, making it easy to identify. It is so bold in appearance that it's difficult to integrate into just any spot. The large leaves resemble a banana leaf, but the fan-shaped manner in which they are joined is what sets the Travelers Palm apart. The name comes from the fact that at the base of each leaf is a cavity that holds water, often used to quench the thirst of weary travelers. The flowers slightly resemble those of a bird of paradise plant. Native to Madagascar, the Travelers Palm has bright, turquoise-blue seeds that appear after the blooms.

Senna alata ❑ ▶
Empress Candleplant or Seven Golden Candlesticks

You may notice a bright yellow bloom, up to 2 feet high, that resembles a candle in shape. This plant, native to tropical America, is easy to spot when in bloom. Flower clusters are mostly unopened buds, which Mexicans call Secret Flower. Given the right conditions, this plant will flower year-round and can reach a height of 15 feet when fully mature.

FUN FACT: One of the oldest sources of medicines in the Americas, Candleplants have provided treatments for skin diseases and ringworm since the days of the Aztecs.

Solandra maxima ❑ ▼
Chalice Vine or Cup of Gold

This fall- and winter-flowering vine has large, showy flowers that are yellow with a purple line through the petal. Native to Mexico, Chalice Vine grows on the edges of sea cliffs and is hardy enough to withstand showers of sea spray. It looks best when trained over a pergola or trellis. The bloom has a nighttime fragrance similar to the scent of vanilla. Left to grow in full sun, it can reach a length of over 30 feet.

Senecio confusus ❑ ▲
Mexican Flame Vine

This plant's bright orange flowers are probably what earned it the name Flame Vine. The flowers are also very fragrant. One of the relatives of this 20-foot-long vine is Dusty Miller, a common bedding plant.

Strelitzia juncea ☐ ◄
Leafless Bird of Paradise

This bird of paradise plant can usually be identified by its distinctive leaves. In this case, however, there aren't many leaves, if any. It more closely resembles a type of rush plant, appearing to have many stems and no leaf blades. The flower, however, looks similar to the flowers of other species of *Strelitzia*. This native of southern Africa thrives in areas that receive quite a bit of sun.

GRASSES

Arundo formisana ☐ ▲

All three of the species in the genus *Arundo* usually grow wild along the rivers and in the ditches of Europe, where it is native. *A. formisana* can be recognized by its bamboo-like foliage. Topping the reed-like stems are feathery terminal spikes. Because it grows so well in the southeastern United States, it appears to be a native.

Eragrostis curvula ☐ ▲
African Love Grass

Throughout the grassland savanna, clumps of 2.5- to 3-foot-tall African Love Grass are planted for the animals to munch on during the day. Many clumps of this plant are also grown in the browse fields to supply the animals with fresh "snack food" every day. This grass is also a fast-growing ground cover.

Cortaderia selloana 'Pumila' ☐ ▲
Pampas Grass

Native to South America, this bushy grass is commonly known as Pampas Grass. The blade is long and tapering, with sharp edges. Flowering is impressive, with tall white plumes towering above the foliage. This grass is grown commercially for dried floral arrangements, and its leaves are used for manufacturing paper.

Miscanthus floridulus □ ▲

American Silvergrass or Japanese Feathergrass

This perennial grass is native to Japan and the Pacific Islands. The seed heads are frequently used in fresh or dried flower arrangements. It also works well in landscaping as a temporary screen or hedge. Over time, this grass will form thick, dense, 7-foot-tall clumps and reddish or purple seed clusters.

Miscanthus transmorrisonensis □ ▲

Evergreen Miscanthus or Evergreen Japanese Feather Grass

This evergreen grass is a perennial native to areas of Asia where snow is likely. Reaching heights of 5 or 6 feet, with clumps as wide as 8 feet, this grass makes a great specimen plant or border plant for a garden. In areas where a lack of water is a concern, *Miscanthus transmorrisonensis* is a perfect choice because it is drought-tolerant and able to live in a wide variety of conditions. Like many other grasses, it is often dried for ornamental purposes.

Muhlenbergia capilaris □ ▼

Hairy Awn Muhly

This southeastern U.S. native can be seen in abundance on the savanna. The blades of this grass grow to about 2 feet and have a fine texture. It is drought-resistant but becomes much more lush with regular watering. Twelve-inch-long pink flower panicles, or stalks, appear on the grass in the fall, giving it a striking appearance. The pink color eventually fades to light brown in early winter.

Muhlenbergia dumosa □ ▲

Bamboo Muhly

Native to southeastern Arizona and northern Mexico, this grass resembles bamboo, hence the common name. The leaf blades are bright green. The small flowers appear in late fall or early winter and have a pinkish cast to them. This plant is often used as an ornamental.

Pennisetum hybrids ❑ ▲
Fountain Grass

Some of the grasses planted at DISNEY'S ANIMAL KINGDOM® PARK are hybrids of *Pennisetum setaceum,* also known as Fountain Grass. Often the seed heads are purple or red. Another member of this genus is *P. americanum,* or Pearl Millet. Millet is a staple food in parts of Asia and Africa. It is sold as a forage crop in the United States and is also a common ingredient in bird food.

Rhynchelytrum repens ❑ ▲
Natal Grass

This perennial grass is native to southern Africa. Over the years, however, it has become naturalized in Florida, Texas, and Arizona. This grass is grown primarily as a meadow grass for grazing, but on some occasions it is used for ornamental purposes.

Saccharum ravennae syn. Erianthus ravennae ❏ ▲
Ravenna Grass

It is not surprising to discover that the *eri* in *Erianthus* means "woolly." You can see that this plume grass has fuzzy or woolly flower spikes. They are silvery-white and are often 12 to 24 inches long. This plant's large, stout stumps have gray-green leaf blades. Ravenna Grass works well both as a specimen plant and as part of a mass planting.

Tripsicum dactyloides ❏ ▲
Fakahatchee Grass

This grass is becoming more popular in the landscaping world because it is easy to grow and remains virtually pest-free. It can reach heights of 5 feet, and the clumps may be as wide as 4 feet. It grows along the U.S. east coast south of New England. It thrives in wet areas, especially along drainage ditches and near bogs.

Thysanolaena maxima ❏ ▲
Tiger Grass

Native to tropical Asia, this perennial grass has roots that remain hardy to temperatures as low as 15°F. The leaves, on the other hand, need protecting, as they fare poorly when the temperature drops. The leaf blades are somewhat coarse in appearance and can reach 3 inches wide. The spikes are dense with flowers. It is cultivated as an ornamental in both California and southern Florida.

Acacia spp. ❏ ▶

There are some 1,200 species of acacia. Most are from the tropical and subtropical regions of Australia and Africa. A few of the many species that can be seen throughout Africa in DISNEY'S ANIMAL KINGDOM® PARK are *Acacia maidenii* (Maiden's Wattle), *A. nilotica* (Gum Arabic), and *A. xanthophloea*. These shrubs and trees have vicious spines and are referred to collectively as "thorn trees."

Acacia maidenii
Maiden's Wattle

A. nilotica is a source of babul gum or gum arabic. It is eaten mixed with sesame seeds, fried in ghee, or used in the preparation of candied flowers, almond paste, and other sweets. The seeds are roasted and used as a condiment or mixed with dates and fermented to become an alcoholic beverage. The tender young pods and leaves are used as vegetables. The flowers are made into fritters. A wine, known as sak, is made from the bark.

Some acacias have been introduced to other countries for economic reasons and have important uses as timber, tanbark, dyewood, gums, and other commercial products. In warmer parts of the United States, particularly on the west coast and in Hawaii, acacias are grown for their showy flowers. These distinct small yellow, cream, or white puff-balls appear on each flush of new growth. They are also very fragrant and produce bee-attracting pollen. The fruits are either round or flattened pods. The hard-coated seeds remain viable for up to 30 years and need to be heated and soaked to germinate. Some even need fire to germinate. At DISNEY'S ANIMAL KINGDOM PARK, acacias grow on the savannas, where they are the preferred food of the giraffes. Watch how they can maneuver their tongues around those thorns and strip off the leaves.

Acacia nilotica
Gum Arabic

Acacia xanthophloea

BROWSE

In the wild, a large portion of a herbivore's day is spent foraging for food. At Disney's Animal Kingdom® Park, animals can be tempted by more than 4 million trees, plants, shrubs, vines, palms, grasses, and ferns representing more than 3,000 species spread throughout the park's 500 acres. However, even though the animal habitats were designed to resemble natural environments and to encourage natural behaviors (like eating), the park's long-term maintenance depended on creating a plan that would keep the animals from munching on all the trees and shrubs in the landscape. The answer? Browse.

Browse is plant material given to the animals for enrichment, as snack food, and as a vital part of their diet. It often consists of shoots, twigs, leaves, and blooms of various plants.

On 94 acres of fields backstage at Disney's Animal Kingdom Park, horticulturists grow a selection of plants that include banana, bamboo, acacia, papaya, and willow. Many of the plants from the browse fields are cultivated in specially designed containers that stimulate root growth. This allows an increase in nutrient uptake, causing the plant to grow larger and healthier in a shorter period of time. Responding to requests from the animal keepers and diet keepers, the browse program delivers 6,500 pounds of foliage per week.

Every day, before the sun comes up, browse teams are out cutting and collecting the requested plant material. Because the plants will be eaten, organic methods are used to process the browse. After collection, the cuttings are submerged in tubs of ice-cold water to keep them fresh and to remove any unwanted insects. After the plants are cleaned, they are tagged with the date, the species that will eat them, and the appropriate location, and then stored in a walk-in cooler in the Forage Warehouse until feeding time.

FUN FACTS ABOUT BROWSE:
- *Not all of the browse is specially grown. In fact, every week the browse team travels more than 200 miles throughout the park collecting plant material like pine cones, willow logs, grape vines, and palm fronds. The browse team even provides 10 pounds of ants every day for our Giant Anteater in The Oasis.*
- *The gorillas on the Pangani Forest Exploration Trail® use the browse not only for food but to make nests as well.*
- *Acacia is a good source of vitamin E for our animals, particularly the rhinos.*
- *Bamboo is a good source of fiber and is low in fat.*
- *Papaya is grown not only as a food item but as a "banker site" to attract beneficial insects.*
- *Herbs are used to encourage the animals to explore their habitats.*
- *Animal impact on the landscape is monitored with the help of a high-tech computerized mapping and analysis tool that projects long-term trends and patterns—including seasonality, animal use, and plant survival—to help our horticulturists better manage the landscape.*

Acrocomia totai ❏ ◀

Gru-gru Palm

Native to northern Argentina and Paraguay, the Gru-gru Palm is not a very friendly-looking plant. Spines circle the entire trunk from top to bottom. The leaflet stalks are also prickly. It is a fast-growing and enormously useful tree—it can be used for building materials or for the production of wine or palm kernel oil, and the fruit is harvested for consumption.

Adansonia digitata ❏ ▶

Baobab Tree

The Baobab Tree is a stunning sight in the tropical African landscape. The tree may grow to have a trunk 30 feet thick; if it becomes hollowed with age, people may use it as a tomb or water tank. Old trees can reach monstrous proportions, often branching near the ground into several hugely swollen trunks, each of which may be 80 feet or more in height. A Baobab Tree often bears the scars of the fires that periodically engulf but do not destroy this tree in its vulnerable habitat. In the winter, it sheds its leaves. Summer brings dramatic white flowers, followed by woody, velvet-covered pods with a dry, acid pulp.

FUN FACTS: In the wild African savanna, the Baobab Tree plays a large role in the circle of life. Elephants gouge the base of the tree to extract its moist pulp. Fruit bat colonies find the tree's 6-inch flowers an excellent source of food. Baboons eat its large, elongated fruit. Birds live in the tree and construct elaborate nests that hang precariously from the highest branches, unreachable by predators. In tropical Africa, the bark yields fiber, young leaves are eaten as a vegetable, and the white pulp of the fruit is a base for a lemonade-like drink and fever reducer.

Aloe spp. ❑ ▶

Many people think of the sticky green stuff they use to soothe a sunburn when they hear the word "aloe." While that is one type, there are actually close to 300 species of aloe. Most are native to Africa, specifically southern Africa. *Aloe bainesii* is a tree form of aloe and can reach heights of up to 60 feet, making it the largest tree aloe. The number of spines, or prickles, varies by type, with *A. bainesii* having only scattered spines. Like most aloes, this plant has showy spikes of flowers—a shade of pink, in this case. Members of the *Aloe* genus are succulents (plants with fleshy leaves and stems used

Aloe ferox
Cape Aloe

Aloe bainsii
Tree Aloe

for water storage) and are not frost-tolerant. Another tree form, *A. ferox*, can reach heights of up to 10 feet. The leaves are blue-green, and the leaf margins are covered with red spiny teeth. These leaves are soaked and cooked as a vegetable or preserved in syrup, flavored with ginger, lemon juice, and the very young shoots of fig trees. *A. ferox* is one of the sources for medicinal aloe. Like other aloes, it has a flower spike with scarlet-orange blooms. Look for *A. bainsii* and *A. ferox* in the Harambe Village area.

Pithecellobium flexicaule ❑ ◀

Texas Ebony

This tree has many interesting features: ½-inch black spines, yellow flowers, zig-zagged twigs, and pod-like fruits. Native to Texas and northern Mexico, it is adaptable to seaside conditions. Although it can reach heights of 30 feet or more, Texas Ebony makes a great patio tree. The blooms appear from spring to fall and are especially abundant the day after a rain.

Schizolobium parahybum ❏ ▽
Guapiruvu or Tower Tree

The Guapiruvu (say that three times quickly!), a valued ornamental tree, is known for its huge feathery leaves and wonderful display of yellow flowers in early spring. Native to Brazil, it is a slender tree with a buttressed trunk, and it can grow up to 100 feet. At DISNEY'S ANIMAL KINGDOM® PARK, the young plants look more like fern trees—umbrellas of leaves grow at the top of slender, unbranched trunks. Occasional cold snaps will prevent this tree from reaching its full size in the park.

Kigelia africana ❏ ▶
Sausage Tree

A Sausage Tree is planted across from the Tusker House Restaurant by the Mombassa Marketplace front entrance. Native to tropical Africa, this tree is cultivated in U.S. tropical gardens as an oddity, growing up to 35 feet with evergreen leaves. It flowers in late winter or summer. Its large, bell-shaped, velvety flowers are dark red. In Africa, the fibrous pulp of the fruit is mixed with sugar, honey, and water to produce beer.

FUN FACTS: The Sausage Tree is pollinated in its native Africa by bats attracted to the smell of the tree's flowers (unpleasant to humans) as they open in the evening. At DISNEY'S ANIMAL KINGDOM PARK, where pollinating bats are in short supply, the plant keepers try to pollinate the flowers by hand with a feather duster, so far without much luck. But maybe someday the curious 2-foot-long, 8-pound, sausage-shaped fruits will appear in abundance, dangling from long cords as they do in their native habitat.

Kigelia flower

Spathodea campanulata ☐ ▶
African Tulip Tree

The *Spathodea campanulata* is native to central Africa, from Sierra Leone and Liberia through Uganda. Equatorial Africa is known for its vast tracts of lush vegetation. The blossoms of the African Tulip Tree push themselves above the canopy, providing a striking contrast to the greenery. Although it is sometimes found in the jungle, where it can reach 80 feet, the African Tulip Tree prefers the surrounding open forests, where it has more room to grow. This fascinating tree was first described by A.M.F. Palisot de Beauvois in 1787. Palisot de Beauvois named the genus from the Greek word *spathe*, or "broadswood," for its curved calyx (the flower's outer whorl, made up of leaf-like petals called sepals). He named the species with the Latin *campanulata*, meaning "bell-shaped," for its flower. The blossoms of this tree are yellow or orange, and in the center of the flower cluster are tightly packed buds resembling a clump of bananas. A few new buds open periodically at the outside of the circle. As they fade and die, new buds open, maintaining the perfect ring shape for a long period. Because the flower buds sometimes contain water, this species has been called the Fountain Tree. Children enjoy squeezing the buds and watching them squirt water. The flowers are followed by long, boat-shaped pods that eventually split open to release masses of winged seeds.

In Florida, the African Tulip Tree blooms two or three times a year, starting in spring. It is evergreen in southern Florida and semideciduous in central Florida, meaning it loses some of its foliage in the winter.

FUN FACTS: African Tulip Tree wood is soft and somewhat brittle and has been used by native Africans to make drums.

ASIA

As you enter the land of Asia, you will come upon the temples and memorial pillars of Anandapur, home to the White-cheeked Gibbon and the Siamang. Continue your walking tour to the Maharajah Jungle Trek area, through the 16th-century Royal Forest of Anandapur. The people of Anandapur and the Royal Anandapur Wildlife and Forestry Authority extend their warmest welcome to you and hope you enjoy your adventure.

male

female

White-cheeked Gibbon ☐ ◀ ▶
Hylobates leucogenys

Of all primates, gibbons (members of the lesser apes family) have the distinction of being the only true brachiators—animals that can swing hand over hand through the trees. Though they do not have tails, they do have long, strong, hooked fingers and manage very well in their Asian forest habitat. Brachiation is a fascinating thing to watch: the gibbon pulls its legs close to its body and then swings like a pendulum, letting go with one hand before grasping on to another tree with the other—almost like being momentarily suspended in space. Accomplished acrobats, they are able to cover distances of up to 30 feet and can adjust quickly from a two-handed swing to a two-legged run, then—spinning around a tree trunk—reach up and fly to a higher branch. Notice that the male is black and the female golden. They are monogamous, which is unusual for most mammals.

FUN FACT: Listen for loud "hoots" that allow gibbons to signal their territory and communicate over long distances.

Siamang ❑ ▶

Hylobates syndactylus
The largest of the gibbon species, the Siamang is recognized by its deep black color and red-brown chin. These apes are accomplished acrobats, able to swing 25 to 30 feet from tree to tree; they can also grasp the trunk of a tree, spin around it, and leap to a higher branch. Not surprisingly, it's their long fingers and toes that enable them to perform these acrobatics. Siamangs are social and monogamous creatures. Although they produce offspring only once every two or three years, both male and female care for the young. The Siamang is the loudest of the gibbons. An inflated sac at the throat enables it to produce sounds that can be heard up to a distance of 2 miles: the sound is used as a warning, to announce the establishment of a territory, or as a mating call.
FUN FACT: Although gibbons are fearless when swinging from branch to branch, they are, like many primate species, far less confident in the water.

Maharajah Jungle Trek

From Anandapur, you can pass through the brick gatehouse that is the entry to the Royal Forest and see the wildlife that has come to live among the ruins of the old royal structures. The animals here appear in the order in which you will see them on the trail.

Malayan Tapir ❑ ▶

Tapirus indicus

Although the tapir resembles a pig, it is more closely related to the horse and rhinoceros. Like them, it has an odd number of toes—four on the front feet (three touch the ground) and three on the back feet—each ending in a hoof-like foot. The Malayan is the largest of the world's four tapir species. The front of the body and the hind legs are black, and the midsection is a creamy white, coloring that provides excellent camouflage in its shady forest habitat. The tapir's long nose is probably its most valuable asset: trunk-like in shape, it is sensitive to touch and smell, and can pull leaves and shoots into the animal's mouth.

FUN FACTS: The Malayan Tapir is an excellent swimmer and stays close to the water to get relief from the heat.

ASIA

Komodo Dragon ❑ ▼

Varanus komodoensis

A highly endangered species of lizard, the Komodo Dragon lives only within the small region of Komodo Island, Indonesia. Being cold-blooded (like all reptiles, their body heat is dependent on their environment), Komodo Dragons spend much of their time moving from sun to shade to regulate their body temperature. They prefer dry monsoon forests and savannas, where they feed on pigs, goats, deer, and other Komodo Dragons. They use their flicking, snake-like tongue to pick up and track scents as far as 2 miles away. Serrated, curved teeth and highly infectious bacteria in the mouth make the Komodo Dragon a formidable enemy.

FUN FACT: The Komodo Dragon is the largest living member of the lizard family, with a record length of 10 feet and a weight of 250 pounds.

Malayan Flying Fox ❏ ▲
Pteropus vampyrus

As you step inside the Community Hall, look for two species of fruit bats hanging among the vines and tree branches on the Bat Cliffs of Anandapur. Look closely: the bats may be wrapped in their delicate wings to preserve body heat, or they may be fanning themselves with outstretched wings to keep cool. One of the largest of the bat species, the Malayan Flying Fox has a wingspan of up to 6 feet. These large, fruit-eating bats are native to the Old World and are endowed with excellent eyesight and hearing. Given its size and weight, the Malayan Flying Fox is unable to launch its flight from the ground, and instead must take off from a height.

FUN FACT: Members of this species can eat up to their body weight in food daily.

Rodrigues Fruit Bat ❏ ▲
Pteropus rodricensis

Like the Malayan Flying Fox, the Rodrigues Fruit Bat is known as a megabat because of its large size. True to its name, this bat is found only on the island of Rodrigues in the Indian Ocean—and eats only fruit. This bat is a strong flier: it can hover over the ground, like a helicopter, before landing and, unlike larger bats that need to start at tree height to become airborne, the Rodrigues Fruit Bat can take off from the ground. Fruit bats are a noisy lot, screaming and screeching as they compete for the best roosting place.

FUN FACT: The fruits they eat make these megabats extremely useful to their environment. They spread fruit seeds that renew the forest.

Elds Deer ❑ ▲
Cervus eldi

These shy, graceful deer come from Myanmar and eastern India. Throughout history they were hunted for food and sport, and only a few thousand remain. They are sometimes called "brow-antlered deer" because of the unusual shape of the buck's antlers, which grow approximately 3.5 feet long, curve outward then upward, and sport at least six points. A velvet covering on the antlers has a blood supply that nourishes the antlers during their growth. Each year, when the antler is fully formed, the blood supply stops traveling to the antler and the velvet shrivels and falls off, leaving only bone exposed. The cycle resumes when a new antler grows. In summer, the male's coat is red with pale brown underparts; in winter, the coat changes to dark brown and white. The female is the same but paler.

FUN FACT: The Elds Deer's hooves are especially adapted to its marshy habitat. The foot is wide, and the hooves spread on the ground to help prevent the feet from sinking.

Asian Tiger ❑ ◀
Panthera tigris

Magnificent tigers now reside safely in the ruins of the old hunting lodge. Weighing in at as much as 675 pounds and measuring up to 10 feet long, the Asian Tiger is a formidable creature of the wild; it is also an endangered species. The pattern of black stripes on orange fur (excellent for camouflage) is different on every tiger. Its large eyes are set on the front of its head (a tiger's night vision is six times better than that of a human); its ears can turn individually and rotate up to 180 degrees; it has long, sharp teeth and claws, and is able to leap almost 30 feet, the length of a school bus. Tigers back up to a tree and spray urine on it to mark their territory.

FUN FACT: A male tiger typically consumes almost three tons of meat a year.

Sarus Crane ❑ ◀

Grus antigone

The Sarus Crane is the world's tallest crane, standing up to 6 feet at maturity. Cranes have a distinctive dancing movement in which they strut about with outstretched wings, bow, and leap into the air. They also throw sticks into the air and catch them as they fall.

Java Green Peafowl ❑ ▼

Pavo muticus

This handsome bird resembles a peacock. The male, especially, is distinguished by a long train of upper tail feathers that rise vertically and fan out during courtship display. His plumage is brilliant green when the wings are folded, and his head sports an upright crest and blue and yellow facial skin. The female is similar to the male, but her legs are shorter and she lacks the long upper tail feathers. The beautiful feathers of the peafowl have attracted hunters over the years, and hunting, together with habitat destruction, has caused a massive reduction in the wild populations of these birds.

White-winged Wood Duck ❑ ◀

Cairina scutulata

This is one of the world's rarest ducks. Its habitat has been largely destroyed, and because of its ample size, it is an easy target for predators.

Blackbuck ❏ ▲
Antilope cervicapra

One of the speediest animals in the world, the Blackbuck is able to run as fast as the Thomson Gazelle (see page 60), 50 miles per hour, outpacing even the tiger. Blackbucks are endangered in their native India but flourish in Argentina and Texas, where they have been introduced. The Blackbuck grazes on grasses, leaves, and field fruits, and favors open countryside and parklands. Adult males stand approximately 2.5 feet at the withers. You can identify the males by their unusual, corkscrew-twisted horns that are almost 2 feet long, almost as tall as the antelope itself.

FUN FACT: On the legs are glands that secrete scents to mark off the Blackbuck's territory and to arouse the female during courtship and breeding.

ANTLERS AND HORNS
The antlers you see on deer are quite different from the horns of antelopes, gazelles, and cattle. Antlers do not grow directly from the skull, as horns do, but are supported on discs of bone. Horns are permanent structures, while antlers are shed every year and regrown. Antlers are solid, made of bare, exposed bone, whereas horns have an outer coating and are often hollow.

Bar-headed Goose ❏ ▶
Anser indicus

This very handsome goose is one of the highest-flying birds in the world. It migrates seasonally over the Himalayas from Nepal to India.

Fairy Bluebird ❑ ▲   **Crested Wood Partridge** ❑ ▲
Irena puella   *Rollulus roul-roul*

ASIA AVIARY

Among the ruins of the Community Hall is an aviary with nearly twice as many bird species as the Africa Aviary. Stay a while and try to see them all, even the ones not pictured here.

Near the entry there is a pond that attracts birds to swim and feed. Here you are most likely to see the New Guinea Masked Plover and the Indian Pygmy Goose.

Among the Psittaciformes, you'll see the colorful, seed-eating Amboina King Parrot, the Plum-headed Parakeet, and the Goldies Lorikeet. And among the doves you can find the Green-winged Dove, Nicobar Pigeon, Papuan Mountain Pigeon, Sulawesi Quail-Dove, Jambu Fruit Dove, Wompoo Fruit Dove, and Pink-necked Green Pigeon.

Keep a watch out for the larger birds underfoot—the Crested Wood Partridge, Great Argus Pheasant, and Green Jungle Fowl.

And try to get a good look at the variety of colorful birds that come into the feeders throughout the aviary: Bartlett's Bleeding Heart, Blue-winged Minla, Dhyal Thrush, Fairy Blue Bird, Golden-crested Mynah, Hooded Pitta, Hoopoe, Indian Blue Roller, Japanese White Eye, Orange-bellied Leafbird, Red-throated Barbet, Silver-eared Mesia, Sooty-headed Bulbul, Spice Finch, Timor Sparrow, Tri-colored Flycatcher, White-collared Kingfisher, White-headed Nun, Yellow-throated Laughing Thrush, and Yellow-vented Bulbul.

Green Jungle Fowl

Golden-crested Mynah ❑ ▲
Ampeliceps coronatur

Orange-bellied Leafbird ❑ ▲
Chloropsis hardwickei

Hoopoe ❑ ▲
Upupa epops

Green-winged Dove ❑ ▲
Chalcophaps indica

White-collared Kingfisher ❑ ◀
Halcyon chloris

Goldies Lorikeet ❑ ▲
Trichoglossus goldiei

Dhyal Thrush ❑ ▲
Copsychus saularis

Amboina King Parrot ❑ ▲
Alisterus amboinensis

Silver-eared Mesia ❏ ▲
Leiothrix argentauris

Wompoo Fruit Dove
❏ ▲
Ptlinopus magnificus

Indian Pygmy Goose ❏ ▲
Nettapus coromandelianus

New Guinea Maske Plover ❏ ▲
Vanellus miles

Indian Blue Roller ❏ ◀
Coracias benghalensis

Great Argus Pheasant ❏ ▶
Arusianus argus

Red-throated Barbet ❑ ▲
Trachyphonus erythrocephalus

Nicobar Pigeon ❑ ▲
Caloenas nicobarica

Jambu Fruit Dove ❑ ▶
Ptilinopus jambu

Yellow-throated Laughing Thrush ❑ ▲
Garrulax galbanus

Japanese White-Eye ❑ ▲
Zosterops japonicus

Sulawesi Quail-Dove ❑ ▶
Gallicolumba tristigmata

Kali River Rapids

After you complete the walk through the Maharajah Jungle, you may want to venture onto the Kali River for a wet ride. As you're waiting in the queue, keep a look out for:

Tokay Gecko ❏ ▶
Halcyon chloris

❏ ▲
Shama Thrush
Copsychus malabaricus

Green-naped Lorikeet ❏ ▼
Trichoglossus haematodus

❏ ▲
Pekin Robin
Leiothrix lutea

Onagadori Jungle Fowl ❏ ▲
Gallus gallus domestic

Bombax ceiba ❑ ▲
Red Silk Cotton Tree

The thorny and swollen trunk of this tree makes it an eye-catcher. It belongs to the silk cotton tree genus; the large capsule-shaped seed pods burst open and spew their fibers into the air. The flowers are brilliant shades of pink, salmon, burgundy, and white. The fruit of *Bombax ceiba* can be cut, dried, and eaten, and the young leaves can be dried and used as a potherb. The fleshy parts of the plant are consumed in soups or used in sauces. *B. ceiba* thrives in warm climates with moist soil.

Brunfelsia pauciflora ❑ ▲
Yesterday, Today, and Tomorrow

This plant and its tubular flowers are indigenous to tropical America. When blooming, *Brunfelsia pauciflora* has a unique form and color that adds a special touch to any tropical landscape. The common name of the plant sounds romantic, but it actually describes the evolution of the blossoms. The flowers open as a deep purple with a white center. Within a day they fade to white. Yesterday, Today, and Tomorrow displays blossoms in several colors, depending on the stage of the bloom.

Caesalpinia pulcherrima ❑ ▲
Dwarf Poinciana or Barbados Pride

Caesalpinia pulcherrima originates from the tropical Americas. This large shrub is easy to recognize by its bright orange, red, and yellow blooms. The flowers appear in the spring and last until fall. The clusters can be up to 2 feet long and can each contain as many as 30 to 40 flowers. This plant will remain green throughout the winter unless there is a freeze. The young seeds can be eaten raw or cooked; the flowers are also cooked and eaten.

FUN FACTS: In India, the plant is the sacred flower of Shiva, a Hindu god. An extract from the wood is used to make ink.

Cestrum aurantiacum ❑ ▼
Golden Jessamine

Cestrum is related to the potato. It is native to Central and South America as well as the West Indies. *C. aurantiacum* is grown as a flowering ornamental. Its leaves are noted for their pungent odor when crushed or bruised. The flowers may be yellow, orange, red, purple, or pink, depending on the species, and release a scent at night.

Chorisa speciosa
❏ ◀

Floss Silk Tree
The Floss Silk Tree, native to Brazil, has large, showy blooms and is a stunning sight in the fall. The reddish-violet flowers resemble a tiger lily bloom. A pear-shaped fruit later replaces the flower. When the fruit dries out and splits open, a silky floss appears (hence the name). The tree's seeds are attached to this floss and are dispersed by the wind. This floss has been used to fill life preservers as well as pillows. If you aren't able to see the blooms of this tree, don't worry—you will still be able to identify it by the thick spines around the trunk.

Clerodendrum philippinum

Clerodendrum ugande

Clerodendrum paniculatum

Clerodendrum spp. ❏ ▲

Clerodendrum includes more than 400 species of trees, shrubs, climbers, and herbaceous plants located primarily in the world's warmer climates. Many *Clerodendrum* species have showy flowers. *C. paniculatum* (or Pagoda Flower), native to Southeast Asia, is striking both in and out of bloom. The leaves are large and glossy, sometimes up to 1 foot in diameter, and the scarlet clusters, up to 18 inches tall, are spectacular. The shape of the flower resembles a Chinese pagoda, hence its common name. The Pagoda Flower is often planted in gardens to attract butterflies. (With blooms that large, they are hard to miss.)

C. philippinum var. *pleniflorum* is a shrub native to eastern China, the Philippines, and the southern islands of Japan, though it is naturalized in the United States and throughout the tropics. It usually grows to between 5 and 8 feet and can have leaves 10 inches long. Its fragrant flowers are pink or white and tend to be about 1 inch across.

C. ugandense (commonly known as the Butterfly Bush or Blue Butterflies) has sprays of two-toned, clear-blue flowers that resemble butterflies. This eastern African native is related to other climbing *Clerodendrums,* such as Bleeding Heart Vine (*C. thomsoniae*).

Erythrina variegata ❑ ▲
Variegated Cockspur

This tree is as useful as it is attractive. Often, coffee and cocoa growers will plant this tree to shade their crops. Some species are used for their medicinal qualities. Young leaves are stemmed and eaten or added to soups, stews, or curries. In Vietnam, the leaves are used to wrap a popular food known as *nem,* a kind of hashed meat. The Variegated Cockspur reaches heights of up to 60 feet and, as the name implies, has variegated leaves. The flowers are striking, since one of the petals tends to be enlarged and boat-shaped. Hummingbirds are frequent visitors to this tree.

Ginkgo biloba ❑ ▲
Maidenhair Tree

The Maidenhair Tree is unusual in many ways. It has been around for hundreds of millions of years and is the only tree in its genus, which is rare. The leaves are two-lobed, and the veins run parallel to the leaf margins; the leaves turn an attractive bright yellow in the fall. This tree tolerates pollution well and is often used as a street tree in large cities. It has become popular and widely cultivated for the extract that is produced from it. *Ginkgo biloba* extract is thought to help reduce memory loss, among other things. Fresh ginkgo seeds are harvested in the fall, roasted, and eaten as a seasonal delicacy; they have a mild, sweet, crisp flavor. The canned or dried seeds are added to soups, stews, stir-fry, and tempura for flavor; the seeds are also a source of edible oil. If you like the unusual, this irregularly shaped tree is a perfect specimen.

Ficus religiosa ❑ ▲
Bodhi Tree or Bo Tree

Unlike many of its *Ficus* relatives, this tree, native to northern India, doesn't produce the characteristic aerial roots common to its genus (aerial roots are roots produced from the stem above the ground). This tree holds significance in the Buddhist religion—the common names Bodhi Tree and Bo Tree mean "tree of awakening." It was under such a tree that Buddha is said to have attained enlightenment. When sacred Bodhi Trees reach a certain age and height they are often decorated with strips of colored fabric to show reverence for their age and structure. Like other *Ficus* species, the Bodhi Tree produces a sticky, milky sap. This tree prefers a moist environment but is fairly drought-tolerant, though when water is in limited supply it will not reach its full height of 100 feet. The blue-green leaves can grow up to 6 inches wide.

Justicia carnea ☐ ▲ and Justicia aurea ☐ ▶

Brazilian Plume

The fluffy pink and yellow blooms of *Justicia carnea* and *J. aurea*, respectively, stand out against the surrounding foliage. The blooms tend to make them popular houseplants. If you haven't guessed from the common name, these plants are native to Brazil, though they grow throughout South America. Take a close look at the stems: they are four-sided. These attractive plants are favorites both indoors and out.

FUN FACT: The fruit of these plants is sometimes mixed with other foods to make an effective bait for rodents.

Megaskepasma erythrochlamys ☐ ▲

Brazilian Red Cloak

The Brazilian Red Cloak is in a monotypic genus (a genus with only one species) that occurs naturally in southern Venezuela. Despite its unfriendly name, it is a great-looking shrub with bright red blooms and has grown immensely in popularity since the early 1990s. Mature specimens can reach up to 12 feet.

Tacca integrifolia ☐ ▲ and Tacca chantrieri ☐ ▼

White Bat Flower and Black Bat Flower

The unusual bat flowers from the jungles of Southeast Asia are increasingly featured as oddities in many gardens. The Black Bat Flower *(Tacca chantrieri)* is one of very few black-flowering plants in the world. From its glossy-green leaves emerge a series of purplish-black flowers that resemble fancy bats, with strange, outwardly curving petals and sepals and long, whiskery appendages. As its name suggests, the flowers of the White Bat Flower *(T. integrifolia)* also resemble bats. In the wild, the bat flower dies down in the dry season and returns when it rains. Look for the bat flower inside the bat aviary.

Sesbania grandiflora ☐ ▲

Scarlet Wisteria Tree

Sesbania grandiflora is a tropical and subtropical tree native to Australia and the tropical Americas. Part of the legume family, it is fast-growing and hardy in the right areas. The flowers of this tree are white, red, and pink and resemble the head of a parrot.

Spathoglotis spp. ❏ ▶

This is one of the terrestrial (having underground roots) members of the orchid family. The flowers of the *Spathoglotis* species and their hybrids range in color from yellow or golden-yellow to purple to white.

Spathoglotis hybrid

Spathoglotis grapette Grape Orchid

Xanthosoma sagittifolium ❏ ▶

Elephant's Ear or Giant Taro

The inconspicuous, greenish-white flowers of this tropical American native can be seen throughout the year. The Elephant's Ear is part of the aroid family and has the aroid's characteristic edible, arrow-shaped leaves. The leaves of a mature plant can dwarf a person. *Xanthosoma sagittifolium* is grown as a vegetable in the West Indies as well as Africa. It's a versatile food source: the tuberous roots can be eaten, but harvesters take from the lateral areas only and leave the main roots; some of the underground stems provide a starchy substitute for rice; others can be peeled and then boiled, baked, pureed in soups or stews, or made into chips, pancakes, or fritters.

Tipuana tipu ❏ ▲

Bride of Bolivia

Across from the marble temple is the "Mother Tipuana tree." More than 100 years ago a naturalist obtained from a South American nursery the seeds of this species and brought them back to western Florida. This tree, grown from the seeds, is the stock plant from which other trees were harvested and introduced into Florida. The *Tipuana tipu* can grow more than 100 feet tall in the forests of its native Bolivia. This tree's 4-inch-long flowers resemble miniature orchids. Larger, older trees are breathtaking when in bloom.

DINOLAND U.S.A.

Cross the bridge from the Harambe Village area, pass the huge Brontosaurus skeleton as you enter the DɪɴᴏLᴀɴᴅ U.S.A.® area, and you will find live animals and plants whose ancestries date back to the prehistorical period when this land was traveled by dinosaurs.

American Crocodile ❑ ▼
Crocodylus acutus
Most crocodiles live in fresh water in warm regions. Usually, large crocodiles spend nights in the water and lie in the sun on land for most of the day. Even though its feet are webbed, the crocodile doesn't rely on them to propel it in the water. Rather, it swims entirely by the serpentine movement of its body and the mighty strokes of its oar-like tail. Although the crocodile operates most efficiently in the water, it can use various gaits on land—sliding slowly on its belly, stepping along with its legs extended, and even galloping for short distances.

FUN FACT: In midday heat, the crocodile keeps cool by lying with its mouth wide open. It has no sweat glands and relies instead on water evaporating from its mouth.

Cape Thick-knee ❏ ▲

Burhinus capensis

Out and about in the evening and resting by day in the Kenyan savannas, Cape Thick-knees feed on insects and small invertebrates, stalking their prey not by swooping down but with a trotting gait. They're also fast runners and equally fast fliers. Both male and female incubate the eggs and care for their young.

Red-legged Seriemas ❏ ▲

Cariama cristata

What's in a name? Not much here: Red-legged Seriemas don't have red legs (they're salmon-colored), but they do have a red bill. This bird's most outstanding feature, however, is the set of permanently raised, slightly stiff feathers at the base of its bill, unusual in South American birds. Also unusual is its call, which is often compared to the sound of a yelping puppy and can be heard several miles away. Seriemas are at home in the woodlands, savannas, and scrub of South America, where they feed on grasshoppers, beetles, ants, spiders, and snakes. Always alert to possible danger, seriemas are quick on their feet, preferring to run from danger rather than fly.

FUN FACT: Seriemas are among the few birds with eyelashes.

DINOLAND U.S.A.

CROCODILES AND ALLIGATORS

Crocodiles have teeth in their lower jaw that fit into notches on either side of the upper jaw. In alligators all the teeth in the upper jaw overlap those in the lower jaw.

Bowenia serrulata
Byfield Fern

Cycas taitungensis
Prince Sago Palm or Emperor Palm

Encephalartos woodii x *natalensis*

Encephalartos arenarius

Encephalartos ferox

Diöon spinalosum
Giant Diöon

Cycads

Cycads are true survivors. They have been around since the time of the dinosaurs, and some have not changed much from then until now. During the time of the dinosaurs, they ranged all over the earth, but with the coming of the Ice Age, cycad populations were restricted to tropical and subtropical regions. They grow in every kind of habitat except swamps and can thrive in full sun to near total shade. Some can even live without soil. Some cycads are extremely limited in their natural range, while others appear to be weeds in the undergrowth. But they all produce brightly colored cones and seeds. Botanists use cone, leaf, and trunk structures to distinguish the different species of cycads. For example, only cycads in the genus *Bowenia* have bipinnately compound leaves. And only *Macrozamia* cycads have a colorful callous at the base of each leaflet.

Cycas revoluta
Sago Palm

GYMNOSPERMS

All the non-flowering plants in the DinoLand U.S.A.® area are related—distant cousins, so to speak. From the Bald Cypress and Bunya Bunya trees to the palm-like cycads, they all share the name "gymnosperm." The more common gymnosperms are pine and cedar trees. "Gymnosperm" is translated as "naked seed," which means that these plants have no fruits to cover the seeds and no flowers to attract pollinators. They depend on other means to get their pollen. Pines and Bald Cypresses use wind for pollination, while the cycads use scent and temperature to attract insect pollinators to their cones; the insects either pick up pollen or drop it off. Male cones may stay on the plant for as long as three months, while female cones will nurture their seeds for as long as nine months. Because of this, female plants generally produce cones once every two years, while males produce cones every year.

Zamia floridana
Florida Arrowroot or Coontie

Zamia pseudoparasitica

Zamia furfuracea
Cardboard Palm

Araucaria bidwillii ❑ ▲
Bunya Bunya
The seed cones of the Bunya Bunya are camouflage-green and almost invisible high in the canopy of the tree. Each cone contains about 100 edible seeds. Mature trees bear huge, pine-apple-shaped cones that weigh up to 18 pounds each and are soaked with a white, sticky resin. From pollination, the cone grows to maturity in about 18 months. The Bunya Bunya comes from the rain forest of southeastern Queensland, Australia, and can grow to 120 feet in height. The tree develops a symmetrical crown as it matures, with many long branches that jut out from the thick trunk and bear flat, dark green, prickly leaves.

LIVING FOSSILS

Living fossils are plants that were first described from the fossil record before they were found living. In other words, they were thought to be extinct. One such plant is the Ginkgo biloba tree (see page 105), which must have first appeared about 300 million years ago and flourished all through the Jurassic and Cretaceous periods. After being described from fossils, the Ginkgo biloba was found growing on temple grounds in China. This ancient tree would have become extinct if it hadn't been planted and maintained by inhabitants of the temple, since the native habitat for the Ginkgo biloba no longer exists.

Alsophila cooperi or Cyathea cooperi ❏ ▲
Australian Tree Fern
This native of the mountain ranges of Australia and Tanzania is a rapid grower and will often reach heights of 50 feet or more in its lifetime. The arching fronds of this plant are up to 12 feet long.

Asparagus densiflorus 'Springeri' ❏ ◄
Foxtail Fern
There are two varieties of this common landscaping plant: *Asparagus densiflorus* 'Springeri' and 'Myersii'. The 'Springeri' fern has small, scale-like leaves. White flowers form along the midrib and are soon followed by bright red berries. Found native in Europe, Asia, and Africa, this fern is often used in flower arrangements.

Taxodium distichum ❏ ▲
Bald Cypress
Some specimens of this giant tree growing in the wild are estimated to be 1,000 years old. The native range for this species is from southern New England to Florida, with the largest population found in Florida. *Taxodium distichum* produces pseumatophores, aerial roots or "knees," which help to supply oxygen to the plant's underground and underwater root system. The leaves on this tree have a fern-like appearance. A good way to identify the Bald Cypress is to look for the reddish bark and the "knees."

CONSERVATION STATION

From the station in the Harambe Village area, take the Wildlife Express to CONSERVATION STATION®. Inside the building are exhibitions about the rain forest, with behind-the-scenes views into how we care for the animals at DISNEY'S ANIMAL KINGDOM PARK®. Around the back is where young and old alike can enjoy contact with animals that have been domesticated. CONSERVATION STATION is where humans and animals meet face to face, to encounter the challenges that lie ahead for the conservation of our environment and to consider ways we can all help.

Exhibitions

Some animals are on exhibition in the main building; others are presented to guests throughout the day. Here are some of the animals you're sure to see on exhibit:

Bearded Dragon ❑ ▼

Acanthdruco barbatus
This member of the lizard family earned its name from the spiny jaw pouch that, when flared, resembles a beard. This display is used to intimidate predators and to advertise territory. Bearded Dragons feed by day on insects, spiders, and vegetation. The Bearded Dragon's habit of basking in the sun in its semi-desert habitat enables it to absorb heat and warm up after cool desert nights.

Golden Lion Tamarin ❑ ▼

Leontopithecus rosalia
This tiny animal, weighing only a half pound, makes its home in the forests of South America. Golden Lion Tamarins spend their days foraging for fruit, flowers, vegetation, and arthropods in the trees. They romp from tree to tree with other tamarins during their active, sometimes rambunctious playtime. This is a monogamous species; what's more, the male assumes equal responsibility for caring for the young, who often stay with their parents long after they are weaned.
FUN FACT: Golden Lion Tamarins are one of the few mammals to be successfully reintroduced into the wild. This complex reintroduction program includes their being introduced first to a "halfway house," where they learn survival skills before being fully released into the wild.

PRESENTATIONS AT CONSERVATION STATION

At CONSERVATION STATION®*, there are frequent presentations on both the small stage in the middle of the building and the Animal Clubhouse stage outside, adjacent to The Affection Section. These presentations offer guests the opportunity to meet our animal keepers and some of the special animals they care for, as well as to learn how we all can help make a positive difference for the environment.*

Two-toed Sloth ❑ ▼
Choloepus didactylus

Everything about the sloth is slow: its pulse, its movement, its respiration and digestion. In the forest these animals sleep an average of 15 hours per day. They spend most of their time in trees. When they do descend from the branches, where they sleep, they crawl along on their bellies at an awkward, slow pace. In fact, they swim better than they walk. The sloth is protected by its long body hair and short underfur, which allows for algae growth—a perfect camouflage. True to its name, the Two-toed Sloth has two clawed toes on its front legs (there are three on the hind legs), which enable it to easily grip the branches on which it spends much of its life—hanging upside down. A newborn sloth spends the first nine months of its life riding on its mother's chest.

FUN FACT: Because a sloth spends most of its time hanging upside down, its hairs grow upward from belly to back, perhaps so the rain will run off its body.

AFFECTION SECTION

The Affection Section area is the only place at Disney's Animal Kingdom® Park where you are encouraged to touch the animals.

Dominique Chicken ❑ ▲
Gallus gallus
Well insulated from the cold with their heavy black-and-white plumage, these chickens were introduced into New England from Sussex, England. Extremely rare, Dominique Chickens can lay eggs all year-round.

FUN FACT: These fowl are sometimes referred to as "grandmothers' chickens," because they were often found on U.S. farms in decades past.

Grade Chicken ❑ ▲
Gallus gallus
This chicken is actually a mixture of several domestic breeds.

Guinea Hog ❑ ▼
Sus scrofa
Smaller than the average pig, Guinea Hogs grow only up to 300 pounds. They are at home in cultivated land in the United States. Guinea Hogs feed mostly on grass, roots, and nuts. Fast runners and good swimmers, they are often kept in yards to keep snakes away from the home and to provide general pest control. Unfortunately, this useful member of the pig family is almost extinct.

African Pygmy Goat ❏ ▲
Capra hircus

African Pygmy Goats are a species of domesticated goat bred in Africa for their milk and meat. They are small animals, usually no taller than 18 inches—adult males may weigh as much as 90 pounds, adult females 70 pounds. Their coats show a range of patterns consisting of blacks, whites, and grays. African Pygmy Goats are sociable animals generally kept in herds.

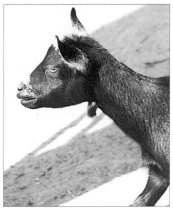

Miniature Donkey ❏ ▲
Equus asinus

The gray or brownish color of the miniature donkey may become more red in the summer. It has been domesticated throughout the world, which is how it continues to exist today.

FUN FACT: When a horse is crossed with a donkey, the result is a mule.

Tunis Sheep ❑ ▶
Ovis aries

Having traveled from northern Africa to the United States in the 1700s in the distinguished company of agriculturists Thomas Jefferson, John Adams, and George Washington, these distinctive-looking sheep are now at home in the United States and Canada. Tunis Sheep have reddish-brown faces and ivory-colored fleece (which turns white when processed), but it is their clean heads and lop ears that set them apart from other sheep. Herbivorous animals, they seek out open cultivated land. Females, called ewes, are very prolific, usually producing twins; they also give large amounts of milk.

Gulf Coast Native Sheep ❑ ▶
Ovis aries

Perfectly suited to the cultivated land of the hot and humid south-eastern United States, Gulf Coast Native Sheep have no wool on their face, neck, legs, or belly—which helps them stay cool in the steamy climate. Most sheep are white; many males (rams) and females (ewes) have horns. Breeding year-round, ewes have one lamb at a time and are very attentive to their young.

FUN FACT: Gulf Coast Native Sheep have a long history: records show that they originated in Spain and were transported to North America by explorers and settlers in the 1500s.

San Clemente Goat ❑ ▼
Capra hircus

Imported from Spain to California's San Clemente Island in the 1500s, these small goats were originally raised for their meat. Now also valued for their milk and fur, they are a very rare breed that nearly went extinct in the 1980s. Today only a few hundred can be found throughout the United States. San Clemente Goats are very sociable and extremely curious, and can adapt to a variety of environments, although as herbivores they prefer grassy pastures. The San Clemente Goat can be very destructive of native landscapes.

Nigerian Dwarf Goat ❏ ▼
Capra hircus

Among the more gentle and graceful members of the animal kingdom, the Nigerian Dwarf Goat was brought from western Africa and is now found in the United States and Canada. It produces up to two quarts of milk a day, has excellent climbing skills, and adapts to a wide range of temperatures. Much like pets (they originally were used as companions), they need regular care: their hooves need to be trimmed every four to eight weeks, and they must be wormed several times a year. Adult males are called bucks; females are does. They weigh between 45 and 80 pounds.

Llama ❏ ▼
Lama glama

A member of the camel family, the Llama is now a domesticated species. Throughout their history, Llamas have been used to carry heavy loads in baskets strapped to their backs. Since they are very sure-footed, they adapt well to the mountainous paths in the Andes. The Llama can transport 50 to 100 pounds 16 miles a day, even at altitudes of more than 16,000 feet, stopping only to feed on the grasses and herbs that make up its diet. Because Llamas are so social, however, they work far better if they are members of a pack.

FUN FACTS: Llamas were used as pack animals as far back as the 16th century by the native people of South America. When the Spaniards invaded, they used Llamas (reportedly 300,000 of them) as beasts of burden.

THROUGHOUT THE KINGDOM

Each of the previous sections focuses on a particular area of the park and lists plants that predominate in that section. The Africa section, for example, features acacias, which are distinctive elements of the African landscape. Many other plants, however, are distributed throughout DISNEY'S ANIMAL KINGDOM® PARK. From The Oasis to Africa to Asia, they contribute their colors, textures, and scents to the park's lush and exotic life.

Alocasia odora 'California'
❏ ◄
Elephant's Ear Plant
This plant has large leaves, hence the common name. Most of the *Alocasia* species like to be in the shade and can be found naturally in the understory of the rain forest. Some of the species produce an edible root called taro, which is similar to a potato. Often the leaves of this plant are deeply lobed.

Bougainvillea spp. ❏ ◄
The "flowers" of the *Bougainvillea* are actually colored bracts (modified leaves); in the center is the small white "true" flower. *Bougainvillea* has been cross-bred into numerous varieties that can vary widely in color, form, and size of bract. Some varieties bloom year-round, while others bloom best in the dry season. Purple and magenta are the most popular *Bougainvillea* colors, but hues ranging from pure white to orange to rich crimson can also be found. Some hybrids even have two colors and are known as "rainbow" *Bougainvilleas*. Though by nature a shrub, *Bougainvillea* can be clipped into a hedge or trained to make a free-standing tree, as well as grow on supports as a vine.

FUN FACT: Bougainvillea is named after the French navigator Louis de Bougainville, who first came across the plant in Brazil during the 18th century.

Crinum asiaticum ❑ ▲
Milk and Wine Lily

With the word *asiaticum* as part of the name, it should come as no surprise that this plant is often found growing in the wild in parts of tropical Asia. The leaves are 3 to 4 inches wide, and they often are said to resemble corn leaves. The flowers are what distinguish them: a flower cluster sets at the top of a thick stalk and will produce up to 20 flowers that are usually quite fragrant. This plant starts from a bulb that can weigh up to 20 pounds.

Dombeya x seminole ❑ ▲

Reaching heights of 12 to 15 feet, this plant is covered with blooms almost year-round. These flowers are 6 inches across and are usually a deep pink/rose color. They also have a sweet, honey-like fragrance. Some of *Dombeya* x *seminole*'s relatives have very large leaves.

Gingers ❑ ◀

All of the different genera of gingers resemble each other in some ways, but there are differences as well. The majority of gingers have striking flower spikes. *Hedychium spp.* are known for their sweet-smelling blooms, making them popular for leis. Some of the other species are used for dyes, perfumes, medicines, and spices.

Curcuma

Hedychium gardenarium

Duranta repens ❑ ◀
Golden Dewdrop

The common name is very descriptive of this shrub. Native to tropical America, the plant produces many golden-yellow berries almost year-round. Often there are so many berries on each branch that the weight causes the branches to have a weeping appearance. Golden Dewdrop quickly makes a tall screen. The clusters of bright blue flowers, which are seen both before and during the fruiting of the shrub, attract butterflies. Some of the stems may have sharp spines.

Galphimia glauca ❏ ▲
Thryallis

The Thryallis, native to the tropical Americas, grows wild in Mexico. It makes a great low-growing screen or hedge because it fills in quickly and can get quite thick. The branches tend to be brittle, so planting it in a heavily trafficked area may not be ideal. This shrub often provides year-round color to the areas where it is planted.

FUN FACT: Galphimia glauca is used in Europe as a homeopathic remedy for hay fever.

Ficus repens ❏ ▲
Creeping Fig or Creeping Ficus

The Creeping Fig, native to Asia and southern Japan, thrives in Florida. It is considered one of the best climbers; once established, it grows very quickly and stays consistently dark green unless there is a heavy freeze. If left to grow, its mature leaves can reach sizes up to 4 inches wide. Like many other members of the *Ficus* genus, it has a milky sap.

FUN FACT: In China, the ripe fruit of the F. repens *is processed into a cold beverage.*

Grewia occidentalis ❏ ▼
Lavender Starflower or Four Corners

This evergreen shrub is not very cold-hardy and prefers temperatures above 45°F. Native to southern Africa, this small shrub can reach heights of 20 feet. It is used for a variety of ornamental purposes and can be cultivated on a trellis, grown against a wall, or trained to form a hedge. The flowers are often purplish pink. The fruit, which is a small berry, attracts birds. The name Four Corners comes from the fact that the fruit has four lobes.

FUN FACTS: Ripe flowers are purplish. The juice is consumed fresh or fermented into an alcoholic beverage.

Hibiscus rosa-sinensis ❏ ▲
Chinese Hibiscus

This is one of the most easy-to-recognize plants in the tropical world. Native to Asia and brought to the West in the 1600s, it will remain ever-blooming as long as the temperature stays warm and it receives enough sun. There are numerous varieties of *Hibiscus rosa-sinensis*. It is the state flower of Hawaii and the national flower of Malaysia, and can be found in many colors.

FUN FACT: In India, red petals of the hibiscus are used for shoe polish.

Heliconia rostrata
Lobster Claws

Heliconia psitticorum
Parrot Flower

Heliconia stricta

Heliconia bihai

Heliconia spp. ❏ ▲

It isn't uncommon to hear the *Heliconia* species referred to as Parrot Flowers or Lobster Claws due to the unusual shape of the bracts (modified leaves) that surround the flowers. The showy red, yellow, and orange bracts we see are actually not the flower. The flower is white or yellow and usually so small it's easy to miss. A more familiar plant with this same feature is the Poinsettia, in which the large, red, petal-like part is the bract and the flower is the small yellow portion in the center. The showy bracts of a *Heliconia* last for a long time, making it ideal as a cut flower. The unusual bracts also make an interesting addition to any landscape that receives ample water and sun.

Hamelia patens ❏ ◀

Firebush

Considered an ever-blooming shrub, this plant puts on quite a show of fiery orange blooms throughout the year. When the temperature drops, the leaves add to the display, turning a red/purple color. If you want to attract wildlife such as birds or butterflies to your garden, consider adding *Hamelia patens*. Butterflies and hummingbirds, as well as many other birds, are attracted to both the fruit and flowers of this plant. Firebush is native to Florida.

Holmskioldia tettensis ❑ ▲
Chinese Hat Plant

What do you think the blooms of this plant resemble? Chinese hats. The bloom has a flat, pink, disk-shaped calyx (outer whorl) that surrounds a small blue flower. Notice also that the flowers grow directly on the branches. Native to the Himalayas, this vine can grow 15 feet in length. Kept in shrub form, it will often reach 6 feet.

Justicia brandegeana ❑ ▲
Shrimp Plant

When spotting these blooms for the first time, you can see why the plant was given its common name. The pink, droopy blooms resemble shrimps. The plant itself is thick and shrubby, and soft to the touch. It is native to Mexico and when placed in full sun will bloom almost constantly. *Justicia brandegeana* makes a lovely addition to most gardens.

Ixora hybrids
❑ ▲

Jungle Geranium

The flowers of this *Ixora* resemble a geranium. Growing native in India and Sri Lanka, the Jungle Geranium can reach a height of 12 feet or more. It often flowers year-round, putting on a show with its brightly colored clusters of red, orange, or scarlet blooms.

FUN FACTS: The name Ixora *comes from* Islawara, *one of the many names for the Hindu god Shiva. Along India's Malabar Coast,* Ixora *flowers are used for temple offerings.*

Lonicera japonica ❑ ◄
Honeysuckle Vine

Native to China and Asia, this plant has been used for medicinal purposes. The blossoms form in pairs and turn from white to yellow before wilting.

Monstera deliciosa ❑ ▶

Swiss Cheese Plant or Split Leaf Philodendron Plant

This Central American native has unusual leaves and edible fruit, which is why some of the other common names for it are Window Plant, Breadfruit, and Fruit Salad Plant. Although it is native to the rain forest, you often will see specimens of this plant indoors, because the shady floor of the rain forest and a home interior have light conditions that are perfect for *Monstera* species.

FUN FACT: The edible fruit resembles an ear of corn but tastes like a combination of pineapple, strawberry, and banana.

Musa hybrids ❑ ▶

Bananas

A wide variety of plants exist within this genus. Banana plants are not trees—they're actually more closely related to the grasses. All have "pseudostems" that die after the plant has bloomed and produced fruit. Most members of this genus are quick-growing, often producing fruit in less than 24 months. Watch out when working with members of the *Musa* genus—they have a sap that stains most fabrics.

Banana plants are a flexible resource and can be used in a number of ways. The fibers from one species, *M. textilis,* are used to make marine cords. Many species are grown because they are edible. One familiar species is *Musa* x *paradisiaca,* which produces most of the bananas sold in supermarkets. *Musa* x *acuminata* also plays an important role in commercial fruit production. Several species of *Musa* are grown back-stage at Disney's Animal Kingdom® Park for browse (see page 85).

Passiflora coccinea ❑ ▶

Red Passion Flower

The twining stems of the *Passiflora* display an abundance of spectacular, long-lasting, exotically shaped, fragrant flowers. The flowers range in color from pale pink to purple-red and the fruits from yellow through purple to black. The plant is a great climber for a trellis, arbor, or fence. It loves a warm climate and is grown under glass in the colder climates of the United States. Several species of passion flower are grown for commercial purposes—for their ornamental flowers and edible fruit, and to make perfume. The pulp covering the seeds can be eaten or used for flavoring beverages and ices.

FUN FACT: Passiflora, native to tropical America, was first named by Spanish friars in America from the Latin passio, *meaning "passion," and* flos, *meaning "flower," in remembrance of Christ's crucifixion.*

THROUGHOUT

Philodendron 'Xanadu' ☐ ▲ and Philodendron selloum ☐ ▶
Cut Leaf and Dwarf Philodendron

Both members of the Arum family (Araceae), these plants are perfect for a tropical garden. They produce a spathe (a shield-like bract) that surrounds the spike flower. Found native in South America, these philodendrons have leaves that range in length from 1 foot to 4 feet. The fruit of the *Philodendron selloum* is edible. Neither plant likes the cold but will re-sprout if the top dies back. They are also relatively short plants, rarely growing higher than 6 feet.

Plumbago auriculata ☐ ▶
Cape Leadwort

Very few plants, especially tropical plants, are blue. *Plumbago auriculata,* or Cape Leadwort, native to southern Africa, is one of the exceptions. The unusual baby-blue to sky-blue color makes this plant a favorite among gardeners. *Plumbago* ensures that its seeds will be dispersed by producing sticky, hairy buds that attach themselves to anything they come in contact with. If you live on the seashore, this plant can tolerate a light salt drift. It's a tough plant and works well as a hedge or to cover a fence, bank, or wall.

Polypodium polypodioides ☐ ▲
Resurrection Fern

The genus name *Polypodium* is derived from the Greek *polypous,* meaning "many-footed." When you spot this fern, tucked into palm trees throughout the park or growing on the branches of a Live Oak or Cypress, check out the fronds. They look like they are made up of many tiny feet. This fern is an epiphyte, meaning that it gets its support from a host. The plant is native to Florida.

FUN FACT: This plant's common name comes from its unusual appearance when dry—it looks dead. (The Resurrection Fern can lose 90 percent of its water and still survive.) Add a little water and the plant springs back to life.

Quisqualis indica ❏ ▲
Rangoon Creeper

Quisqualis is native to Myanmar. It is a large, quick-growing vine cultivated throughout the tropical areas of the world for its showy blooms. The blooms are often found in clusters, sometimes up to 12 per cluster, and the color ranges from white to pink to red. They are long, tube-like flowers with an unusual scent. If left unchecked, a *Quisqualis* can easily grow out of control. The leaves can reach a size of up to 6 inches. Training it to climb a trellis or pergola is the best way to enjoy this vine.

FUN FACT: A botanist who was astonished to see this plant transform itself from a self-supporting shrub into a climbing vine named it Quisqualis, *which means "who, what?" in Latin.*

Schefflera actinophylla or Brassaia actinophylla ❏ ▲
Queensland Umbrella Tree

There are more than 700 species in this genus of plants. Native to Australia and New Guinea, the *Schefflera* has become popular both indoors and out. Throughout the world, it is used as an indoor foliage plant because of its bold, tropical appearance. Another common name for this *Schefflera* is Octopus Plant, because of the unusual appearance of its flower stalks. The bright red, 32-inch-long panicles (branched flower stalks) can give the appearance of an octopus sitting on top of a tree. The large (up to 2 feet long), dark green leaves add to the plant's bold look.

Senna spectabilis 'Golden'

Senna spp. ❏ ▶

The genus *Senna* includes about 260 species of evergreen and deciduous trees, shrubs, and perennials from semi-desert, scrub, and savanna in dry, tropical, and temperate regions. Plants in the *Senna* genus are used to produce the purgative drug senna. *S. splendida* is native to southern India and produces showy flowers on a tree that can grow to 75 feet. Another species' name, *spectabilis,* accurately suggests that tree's showiness. The flower panicles are up to 2 feet long and covered with many golden-yellow, bowl-shaped flowers. Usually this plant thrives in the moist woodland areas of Central and South America, where it is native. *S. surenttensis* is referred to as the Scrambled Egg Tree. It produces showy, golden-yellow flowers off and on throughout the year. The common form of this plant is as a small tree or large shrub.

Senna splendida Golden Wonder

Senna surenttensis

Spathiphyllum 'Sensation'® ❑ ◀
Peace Lily
Commonly called spaths, these plants are among the best known in the interior plant industry. They are great pollution fighters and are often used for their ability to "clean up" an office environment. The leaves of the plant remain a very dark green unless they are seriously neglected. In the tropical Americas and the Philippines you would find this plant while walking on the floor of the jungle. The flower or "spathe" is white and stands upright.

Strelitzia reginae ❑ ◀
Bird of Paradise
Native to southern Africa and a member of the banana family, the flowers of this plant are pollinated by birds. The blossoms are protected in a green sheath and emerge one at a time for several days.

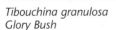

Tibouchina granulosa
Glory Bush

Tibouchina spp. ❑ ▲
Native to Brazil, these attractive shrubs can be recognized by their bright blooms and unique, four-sided stems. The five petals of each flower range from royal purple to pink to white. In the heat of the summer, and also again as temperatures cool, the margins of the leaves turn from green to a reddish or orange color. The new growth is also covered by a reddish fuzz.

Tibouchina urvilleana
Glory Bush

Tibouchina heteromalla
Glory Bush

Bauhinia blackeana

Bauhinia galpinii
Red Bauhinia

Bauhinia tomentosa
St. Thomas Tree

Bauhinia variegata 'Candida'
White Bauhinia

Bauhinia spp. ❏ ▲

This genus of about 250 trees and shrubs native to India and China was named after twin brothers Johannes and Caspar Bauhin, 16th-century Swiss botanists. The two brothers are represented by the unusual, two-lobed leaves. The leaf is easy to identify because it looks like an ox hoof or a butterfly. Plants in this genus bear purple, red, or white orchid-like flowers in the winter to early spring. Later a heavy crop of flat seedpods snaps open, scattering seeds. The flowers, young leaves, and seedpods of some species are eaten as vegetables with rice or in soups, or used as a flavoring in other foods.

Calliandra haematocephala ❏ ▶

Powder Puff
An eye-cathing beauty, this species is native to Madagascar and the tropical regions of India and Africa. Grown for its beautiful flower heads, *Calliandra* has numerous long stamens that give the flower its characteristic powder-puff look. The tree's leaves "fold up" during stormy weather and overnight.

BAMBOO

Bamboo, a member of the grass family (Gramineae) is planted almost everywhere you look in DISNEY'S ANIMAL KINGDOM® PARK. As you walk throughout the park, you can see the new bamboo shoots peeking out above the landscape.

Bamboo existed on Earth 100 to 200 million years before humans arrived, making it one of our planet's most primitive grasses. The bamboo genus consists of 1,200 to 1,500 species. Bamboo is found on every continent except Europe and Antarctica. Bamboos generally fall into the category of either "clumper" or "runner."

CLUMPERS

Many of the tropical bamboos are clumpers; they form a dense, tight clump of vegetation that puts out new shoots in a small area. Members of the **Bambusa** *and* **Dendrocalamus** *genera fit into the clumper category.*

- **B. vulgaris** *is the most common bamboo planted. There are many cultivars of this species, such as* **B. vulgaris** *'Vittata' (or Golden Hawaiian Bamboo) and* **B. vulgaris** *'Wamin.' Although not the most attractive of all the bamboos, this versatile species is economically important and has*

Bambusa vulgaris 'Vittata'

Bambusa vulgaris 'Wamin'

many uses—as a food source and as an all-purpose raw material for products as varied as fishing poles, scaffolding, and musical instruments.

Bambusa oldhamii

  Native to India, it can grow 50 to 60 feet in height. Many of the **Bambusa** *species are also valuable for erosion control and as specimens in the landscape.*
- **D. asper,** *or Giant Clumping Bamboo, can grow as tall as 100 feet with a culm (stem) diameter of 8 inches. This hardy bamboo can also grow in high altitudes. Its large culms are used as building materials and for outriggers on fishing boats. It is also grown for shoot production.*
- *The pale green* **B. oldhamii** *is native to China and Taiwan. Not known to grow in the wild, it is widely cultivated for its edible shoots and as a windbreak. It can reach 55 feet in height. A fine, white powder that covers new shoots remains for one year.*

RUNNERS

A running bamboo sends out runners, or rhizomes, under the surface of the soil that produce new shoots at varying intervals. Keeping these plants under control can be difficult because you never know where the next shoot might pop up.

- **Phyllostachys vivax** *is a bamboo that falls into this category. It can be recognized by the white powdery band beneath each node. All of the* Phyllostachys *bamboos are prized for their elegant form and foliage. They are often used for screens, containers, and specimen plants, or as part of a woodland garden.*

BAMBOO FUN FACTS:

- *No matter where they are planted, most bamboo plants originating from the same population will flower, produce seed, and die at the same time as each other. This means that a clump of bamboo removed from a stand of* **Dendrocalamus asper** *and replanted in a new location will flower, set seed, and die when the bamboo in the original stand does. Most bamboos, regardless of genus and species, mature in this unusual manner.*
- *Bamboo is a plant in a hurry. The fastest-growing plant was clocked speeding upward at 47 inches in a 24-hour period. That's nearly 2 inches per hour.*
- *Bamboo comes in many shapes and sizes. While some of the species reach heights of only a few inches, others tower up to 120 feet. Bamboo attains its height by growing a "horizontal truss" (a joint or node) at distances carefully determined by stress levels in the ascending culm (the stalk or stem).*
- *The cane or culm of bamboo rivals steel in its ability to withstand forces of up to 52,000 pounds per square inch.*
- *The Giant Panda feeds on bamboo almost exclusively. The leaves and stems are a particular favorite.*
- *Bamboo is one of the most widely used natural resources in the world. There are more than 1,500 recorded uses of bamboo in Asia alone. The number of uses worldwide may be greater than 5,000. No other natural resource even compares. Thomas Edison used bamboo to make the filament for the first lightbulb. Alexander Graham Bell used bamboo to make the first phonograph needle. Ninety percent of the paper in India comes from bamboo pulp. Many remedies in Chinese and Asian medicine are derived from bamboo.*

Phyllostachys vivax

Dendrocalamus asper

Cinnamomum camphora □ ▲
Camphor Tree

The Camphor Tree is native to Japan, Taiwan, and Malaysia and can grow as tall as 100 feet. The bark is cinnamon-colored when young and turns gray to brown as the tree ages. New growth is a lovely pink and bronze color and appears from late winter to early summer. When the leaves of this tree are crushed they give off a slightly medicinal odor. The tree's wood, leaves, and twigs are distilled to produce an oil used to flavor food, candy, and beverages. The wood is also used to make cabinets and chests. The Camphor Tree is often planted as a shade tree even though the berries are a nuisance.

Eucalyptus camaldulensis □ ▲
Eucalyptus River Red Gum

Trees in the *Eucalyptus* genus fall into five different categories: gums, bloodwoods, pepperwoods, stringy barks, and ironbarks. Most people are familiar with the eucalyptus oil that is produced by these trees. It is a common ingredient in cough drops and other cold medicines. Tannins (substances used to produce leather) are also obtained from this group of trees. *Eucalyptus camaldulensis* is native to Australia. The bark tends to be quite showy, making this tree desirable as an ornamental as well as for its oil.

Jacaranda mimosifolia ☐ ▶
Jacaranda

The name "Jacaranda" derives from Old World Portuguese. *Jacaranda mimosifolia* is native to the high plains of north-western Argentina, Brazil, and Paraguay, and is a widely planted and admired warm-climate tree. It yields richly figured timber but is valued so highly as a street tree that it is rarely harvested for its wood. The Jacaranda was one of the first trees to be imported to the United States from the tropics.

Jacaranda will reach heights of 50 feet, with fern-like foliage. Depending on the climate, the leaves may shed in the winter or early spring before the flowers.

The blue flowers of the Jacaranda are a rare exception in the plant world, where red, yellow, and white flowers predominate. The Jacaranda is world-renowned for its showy clusters of blue, trumpet-shaped flowers—as many as 40 to 80 flowers can be borne on a single stem. Interesting flat, leathery seed pods follow. Lilacs signal spring in northern areas, and the Jacaranda does the same in Florida.

Erythrina x bidwillii ☐ ▶
Coral Tree

Erythrina x *bidwillii,* or the Coral Tree, originated in Australia in the 1840s from a family of more than 100 species of mostly deciduous tropical trees, shrubs, and herbs. Because of its arresting flowers, the Coral Tree is grown in warm countries as an ornamental. The trunks and branches are protected by short prickles. Some *Erythrinas* are native to North and South America, others to Australia, Africa, and eastern Asia. In areas with a dry season, such as Thailand, northern Malaysia, and most parts of Indonesia, the tree sheds its leaves for a short time. Just as new growth starts, it is covered with a mass of scarlet flowers that attract hummingbirds. Large cuttings will easily root and become sizable trees. Some species have economic value—trees are planted for shade; flowers are cooked and eaten; seeds are made into necklaces; and some seeds have medicinal properties. The Coral Tree is also known as the Dadap and the Tiger's Claw, the latter for the shape of the flowers.

Koelreuteria elegans ☐ ◀
Golden Rain Tree

In the fall, blooming Golden Rain Trees become a focal point of landscapes across Disney's Animal Kingdom® Park. The flowering trees can be easily recognized by the spikes of yellow flowers that stand above the dark green leaves. The flowers are followed by big, showy clusters of pink seedpods. The Golden Rain Tree is native to Taiwan and Fiji. The genus name, *Koelreuteria,* honors Joseph Koelreuter, a natural history professor at the University of Karlsruhe in Germany in the late 1700s.

Magnolia grandiflora ❑ ▲
Magnolia

This genus, named for French botanist Pierre Magnol, contains at least 100 species. Native to the Americas and eastern Asia, the Magnolia is a southern state favorite and can grow 70 to 80 feet in height. The large and creamy-white flowers are followed by a cone-like fruit. Magnolias like deep, rich soil and don't transplant easily, so be careful of the delicate roots if you try.

FUN FACT: In some parts of England, magnolia flowers are considered a delicacy and are used as a spice or in condiments.

Peltophorum dubium ❑ ▲
Copperpod

This popular garden tree is virtually maintenance free. Grown for its shade and its flowers, it is also called the Yellow Flame Tree. The bright yellow flowers, which appear in erect clusters, are very dense.

The leaves fall for a short time during the dry season, and velvety-brown flower buds appear along with new growth; the flowers continue after the tree is fully leafed, creating an attractive mixture of yellow and green. Then masses of thin, flat, copper-colored pods appear, each holding three or four seeds, hence the tree's main common name.

Native to coastal Malaysia and tolerant of most conditions, the tree is often planted along avenues and parks for shade. The bark is used in Java to make a dark brown color for dyeing batik cloth.

Quercus geminata ❑ ▲
Sand Live Oak

What makes this tree interesting is its ability to thrive in very sandy soil. *Quercus geminata* is a scrubby tree with little commercial value. It can be found in the coastal regions of many southern U.S. states from Virginia to Florida. It prefers the understory of a Slash Pine ecosystem.

Quercus virginiana ❑ ▲
Southern Live Oak

This tree grows wild in North America south of Virginia. Due to its very large size, it is often thought to be one of the most beautiful and impressive members of the *Quercus* (oak) genus. Specimens have been found that are more than 2,000 years old. The crown spread can reach more than 200 feet in diameter, with many trees having a trunk more than 8 feet wide. The pollen from these trees tends to be a primary cause of hay fever in the spring. *Q. virginiana* is adaptable to many different climates, even to areas near the ocean where the air and water tend to be salty. The acorns of this tree are used for hog feed and are a food source for animals in the wild.

Tabebuia spp. ❑ ▶
Trumpet Trees

Tabebuia includes about 100 species of shrubs or trees native to tropical America. *Tabebuias* are among the most common and showy flowering trees in the New World tropics and subtropics and are particularly useful as street trees or specimen trees. In the United States, *Tabebuias* are mostly grown in Florida. Spectacular clusters of trumpet-shaped flowers are borne on bare branches in the early spring, making it easy to remember the common name of this beautiful tree. The yellow-flowering species is called the Golden Trumpet Tree, and the pink/lavender-flowering species is the Lavender Trumpet Tree. Several species reach heights of 50 to 60 feet and yield excellent timber. The posts that hold up the mesh of the Africa Aviary are made of this timber.

THROUGHOUT

Bismarckia nobilis ❑ ▲
Bismarck Palm

Named for Prince Bismarck, this palm is one of the most desirable for subtropical landscapes. Due to its large size (in its native Madagascar the Bismarck can grow to 100 feet), in the wrong place it can dwarf everything around it. The foliage is a blue-green color.

PALMS
Most palms are tropical or subtropical. In nature they grow not only in solid stands but also with other plants. Each species has distinctive bark and leafing characteristics, but in general palms tend to grow tall and are topped with graceful fronds.

Livistona chinensis
❑ ◄

Chinese Fountain
This palm is from China and Japan. The fronds are split and drooping and will almost form a screen. The trunk is rough. The fruits are a rosy gray to grayish blue.

Phoenix canariensis □ ▶

*Canary Island
Date Palm*

Found native only on the Canary Islands, this palm is a very impressive addition to a landscape. It can reach heights of 40 feet, with leaves that are between 10 and 20 feet long. Because its trunk is so straight, it is perfect for lining an avenue or boulevard. *Phoenix canariensis* is a relative of the date palms, but the fruit, although edible, is not very tasty. Out of all the members of the *Phoenix* genus, *P. canariensis* is the most hardy and the largest. It is also, to a certain extent, tolerant of salt water.

Phoenix dactylifera □ ▲

Date Palm

This attractive palm tree, with its blue-green, feather-shaped fronds, is thought to have been cultivated for several thousand years. It is one of the staple foods in northern Africa, where is it believed to be native. Although drought-tolerant, these palms are always found near an oasis in the desert. They produce edible fruit and are a source of timber.

Phoenix roebelinii □ ▲

Pygmy Date Palm

Like its relative *Phoenix reclinata* (following page), the Pygmy Date Palm is often found in clusters. It is a small plant and grows only to about 6 feet. Native to Vietnam, Laos, and Cambodia, *P. roebelinii* is found in the tropical rain forests. The fronds are very delicate-looking. It is commonly used in landscaping, with two or three individual plants potted together in a cluster.

Phoenix reclinata □ ▲
Senegal Date Palm

Adding this plant to any landscape will instantly give a tropical feel to the area. This palm usually forms clusters with curving trunks. In fact, it is rare to find a *Phoenix reclinata* with a straight trunk. Native to tropical Africa, it loves water. Using this cluster palm for a hedge works well as long as the water-drawing roots are allowed to develop. The seeds are used as a coffee substitute. The terminal buds of the Senegal Date Palm are used as a vegetable, and the raw ripe fruits are sweet and tasty.

Phoenix sylvestris □ ▲
Wild Date or Indian Date Palm

Native to India, this palm is less stiff than its relative, the Canary Island Date Palm on the preceding page. *Phoenix sylvestris* adds a tropical appearance to any landscape. A common nickname is "Toddy Palm." In India, the sap of this plant is a great source of palm sugar. The sap can also be fermented to make an alcoholic beverage.

Syagrus romanzoffiana ☐ ▽
Queen Palm

The fronds of this palm resemble huge ostrich feathers. Native to Brazil, the Queen Palm is one of the fastest-growing palms in the world (up to 2 feet per year is not uncommon). The arching fronds give the plant an extremely elegant look. Although usually grown strictly for ornamental purposes, palm kernel oil can be produced from the fruit.

Washingtonia robusta ☐ ◀
Mexican Fan Palm

This palm is easy to recognize. Often the dead fronds are left hanging from the crown. This gives the appearance of a petticoat or a hula skirt. This quick-growing plant is native to Baja California and the Sonoran Desert of Mexico and is becoming a favorite among landscapers. The base of the fronds is usually covered with many fine teeth. In California, the dead fronds have to be removed because they are a fire hazard.

Wodyetia bifurcata ☐ ◀
Foxtail Palm

This Australian native was unknown to botanists and horticulturists until the early 1980s. Despite its recent discovery, it is now a very popular palm because it grows quickly and is attractive. The Foxtail Palm tolerates a wide range of soils and prefers ample moisture. The flowers are not very beautiful, but the clusters of orange or red fruits make up for the blooms. This palm looks best forming the upper layer of a woodland canopy.

THROUGHOUT

M

Macaw
- Blue-and-yellow, 34
- Green-winged, 34
- Hyacinth, 12
- Military, 12
- Scarlet, 13

Mandarin, 17
Mandrill, 54, 55
Masked Plover, New Guinea, 100
Meerkat, Slender-tailed, 75
Merganser, Hooded, 17
Mesia, Silver-eared, 100
Muntjac, Reeves, 15
Mynah, Golden-crested, 99

N

Nyala, 48

O

Okapi, 49
Oryx, Scimitar-horned, 65
Ostrich, 64
Otter, Asian Small-clawed, 31

P

Parrot
- African Grey, 69
- Amboina King, 99

Partridge, Crested Wood, 98
Peafowl, Java Green, 96
Pelican
- Pink-backed, 50
- White, 55

Pheasant, Great Argus, 100
Pigeon, Nicobar, 101
Pintail
- Bahama, 18
- Northern, 53
- White-cheek, 18

Plover, New Guinea Masked, 100
Pochard, Rosybill, 18
Psittaciformes, 12
Pygmy Goat, African, 117
Pygmy Goose
- African, 69
- Indian, 100

Q

Quail-dove, Sulawesi, 101

R

Rhinoceros
- Black, 46
- White, 67

Robin, Pekin, 102
Roller
- Indian Blue, 100
- Racquet-tailed, 70

S

Secretary Bird, 60
Seriemas, Red-legged, 109
Sheep
- Gulf Coast Native, 118
- Tunis, 118

Shelduck, Radjah, 19
Siamang, 92
Slider, Yellow-bellied, 9
Sloth, Two-toed, 10, 115
Spoonbills, 37
- African, 10
- Roseate, 38

Spotbill, Indian, 17
Starlings, 70
- Amethyst, 70
- Emerald, 70
- Golden-breasted, 70
- Superb, 70

Stifftail, 18
Storks, 37
- Abdim's, 36
- Hammerkop, 71
- Marabou, 74
- Painted, 37
- Saddle-billed, 37, 51
- White, 36
- White-bellied, 36
- Woolly-necked, 36
- Yellow-billed, 51

Swan, Black-necked, 11

T

Tamarin
- Cotton-top, 30
- Golden Lion, 114

Tapir, Malayan, 93

Principal Photography: Susan E. Meyer.

Others:

D. Allen Photography/Animals Animals: Waterbuck, 66

Mark N. Boulton/Photo Researchers, Inc.: Black Rhinoceros, 46–47

Ruth Cole/Animals Animals: Northern Pintail, 53

Studio Carlo Dani/Animals Animals: Stanley Crane or Blue Crane, 50

Nigel Dennis/Photo Researchers, Inc.: Yellow-billed Duck, 53

Michael Dick/Animals Animals: Bearded Barbet, 71; Golden-crested Mynah, 99; White-cheeked Gibbon (male), 90

The Walt Disney Company: African Elephant, 60–61; African Lion (male), 62; African Lion (female), 63; Axis Deer, 31; Cheetah, 62; Cotten-top Tamarin, 30; Grant's Zebra, 56-57; Gunther's Dik Dik, back cover, 74; Komodo Dragon (both) 93; Mandrill (both), back cover, 5, 54; Malayan Flying Fox, 94; Nile Crocodile, 52; Nile Hippotamus, 52–53, 53, 72–73; Nyala, 48; Okapi, 49; Ostrich, 64; Patterson's Eland, 56; *Peltophorum dubium* (Copperpod), 134; Red Kangaroo, 35; Reticulated Giraffe, front cover, 1, 58, 85; Rodrigues Fruit Bat, 94; Sable Antelope, 59; Thomson's Gazelle, 60; *Tipuana tipu,* 107; Western Lowland Gorilla (both), 75; Yellow-billed Stork, 51

Derek Fell: *Bambusa oldhamii,* 130; *Jacaranda mimosifolia* (Jacaranda), 133; *Lagerstroemia indica* (Crape Myrtle), 42; *Lonicera Japonica* (Honeysuckle Vine), 124; *Magnolia grandiflora* (Magnolia), 134; *Plumeria* hybrid (Frangipani), 25; *Tabebuia* spp. (Trumpet Tree), 135

Aaron Ferster/ Photo Researchers, Inc.: Babirusa (head): 11

Kenneth W. Fink/Photo Researchers, Inc.: Parma Wallaby, 14; Tufted Deer, 15; Yellow-backed Duiker, 49

Michael Fogden/Animals Animals: Helmeted Guinea Fowl, 47

Mickey Gibson/Animals Animals: Cape Thick-knee, 109

Eric Hosking/Photo Researchers, Inc.: Babirusa, 11

Cathy and Gordon Illg/Animals Animals: Hooded Merganser, 17

Tom and Pat Leeson/Photo Researchers, Inc.: Golden-breasted Starling, 70

Jeff Lepore/Photo Researchers, Inc.: Bufflehead, 16

Joe McDonald/Animals Animals: Lady Ross's Turaco, 71

Tom McHugh/Photo Researchers, Inc.: Bongo, 48

Anthony Mercieca/Photo Researchers, Inc.: Emerald Starling, 70

Steven David Miller/Animals Animals: Wompoo Fruit Dove, 100

John Mitchell/Photo Researchers, Inc.: Ruddy Duck, 18

S. Osolinski/Animals Animals: Impala (male), 57

William M. Partington/Photo Researchers, Inc.: Florida Chicken Turtle, 19

Jerry Pavia: *Gardenia jasminoides,* 41; *Strelitzia reginae,* 128

Andrew Rakoczy/Photo Researchers, Inc.: White-cheeked Gibbon (female): 91

A.H. Rider/Photo Researchers, Inc.: Ringed Teal, 18

Len Rue, Jr./Animals Animals: Secretary Bird, 60

Len Rue, Jr./Photo Researchers, Inc.: Ruppell's Griffon Vulture, 65

Jany Sauvanet/Photo Researchers, Inc.: Giant Anteater, 14–15

Bill Silliker, Jr./ Animals Animals: American Crocodile, 108–109

R. Van Nostrand/Photo Researchers, Inc.: White-collared Kingfisher, 99

Joseph Van Wormer/Photo Researchers, Inc.: Red-throated Barbet, 101

Peter Weimann/Animals Animals: Fairy Bluebird, 98

Jeanne White/Photo Researchers, Inc.: Golden Lion Tamarin, 114

Jack Wilburn/Animals Animals: Japanese White-Eye, 101

Roger Wilmshurst/Photo Researchers, Inc.: Puna Teal, 19